The BAD for YOU COOKBOOK

CHRIS MAYNARD & BILL SCHELLER

VILLARD BOOKS ▓ NEW YORK • 1992

To Carrie Maynard, Philomene Lavallee, Lillian Scheller, and
Euphemia Marchitti

VILLARD BOOKS is a registered trademark of Random House, Inc.

Grateful acknowledgment is made to the following for permission to reprint
recipes: JEFF SMITH: Cassoulet Corpulent recipe copyright © 1990, The
Frugal Gourmet, Inc., Seattle. JANE AND MICHAEL STERN: Raparees recipe
copyright © Jane and Michael Stern, with thanks to Ben Van Vechten.

Library of Congress Cataloging-in-Publication Data
Maynard, Chris
    The bad for you cookbook/by Chris Maynard and Bill Scheller.—
1st ed.
        p. cm.
    ISBN 0-679-73545-3
    1. Cookery. I. Scheller, William. II. Title.
TX714.M378 1991
641.5—dc20 91-28109

Manufactured in the United States of America

98765432

First Edition

Design by Robert Bull Design

"Sooner or later in life,
we all sit down to a banquet of consequences."
—ROBERT LOUIS STEVENSON

CONTENTS

•

INTRODUCTION

*It's Time to Get In Touch with Your Dinner;
or,
Why Can't We Just All Sit Down and Eat?*

●

"That all-softening, overpowering knell,
the tocsin of the soul—the dinner bell."
—BYRON, *Don Juan*
"Without fat, a pastrami sandwich
is a worthless commodity."
—JACKIE MASON

WE HAVE STOPPED listening to our poets and sages. Nowadays, instead of listening for the tocsin we are looking for the toxins, and the Food Police will not be happy until the pastrami has gone the way of the fat.

What happened? How did old-fashioned church suppers ironically become what the *Baltimore Catechism* used to call a "near occasion of sin?" How did the fat get bred out of hogs to the point where you'd have to render three counties in Iowa to get a pound of lard? How did the beef producers get pushed into running what look like ads for china plates decorated with meat smidgens?

Enlightened modern types, by which we mean those who invariably do what they're told when they hear the words "It's good for you" (and who probably used to remind the teacher to give out the homework assignment) will have no problem answering these questions. They know that after millions of years of merrily feeding our faces, we've learned that most of what we've been feeding them has been killing us. After all, aren't most of the people who have ever lived dead? Must have been something they ate.

But we suspect that there's another reason why Jackie Mason worries someone will take the fat out of his pastrami. It has to do with the cuckoo religion that a band of dyspeptic Englishmen brought to Massachusetts almost four hundred years ago: its cultural heirs actually *enjoy* being told that stuff they like is bad for them. For a long time, to paraphrase a line of Mencken's, Puritans spent so much time worrying that someone, somewhere might be enjoying sex they tended to overlook the sin of eating with gusto, but they never overlooked it entirely.

One of us—the one who is half Italian, and thus a hopeless dietary unregenerate in the eyes of the righteous—used to have a girlfriend who had been raised by Baptists. She turned out all right on most accounts (although so did Romulus and Remus after being brought up by wolves), but she always had this thing about discussing food too elaborately while you were eating it, or recalling past meals in too much detail. Her mother and father, you see, had discouraged the bad habit of making too much fuss over a mere necessity of life, of turning fuel for the day's work into a source of pleasure.

Those good Baptists, of course, were only creating a policy on food from an overall worldview that had little use for dancing, movies, drinking, gambling, and books in which people took off their clothes. They probably wouldn't have admitted to having a food policy; they'd just say they ate, and said grace beforehand. But the history of American Puritanism is full of people who made a living out of nattering at their countrymen about what to eat, or what not to eat. In the early nineteenth century, Sylvester Graham—he of the flour that begat the cracker—weighed in against pie, of all things. Graham said that Americans were ruining their health by eating pie, and since we have to assume he was including apple, we can count him as one of the country's first true subversives. Toward the end of the 1800s, we had to listen to the likes of Dr. John Harvey Kellogg, who once wrote a paper with the delightfully ambiguous title: "Nuts May Save the Race." It was Kellogg who, in another treatise called "Plain Facts for Young and Old," laid down the following dictum:

> A man that lives on pork, fine-flour bread, rich pies and cakes, and condiments, drinks tea and coffee, and uses tobacco, might as well try to fly as to be chaste in thought.

Chaste in thought! Here, in one of Kellogg's beloved nutshells, is the main message of the Food Police—a message that transcends simple Puritanism. Its appeal to reformers of all stripes is evidenced by its remarkable similarity to an utterance of the poet Shelley, a man we seldom think of as a straightlaced Calvinist. "I hold," Shelley wrote in his 1813 "Vindication of Natural Diet," "that the depravity of the physical and moral nature of man originated in his unnatural habits of life."

And so down to our own day. We recently were browsing through *Living the Good Life*, an annoying little polemic on How One Ought to Behave written by Helen Nearing, widow and coconspirator of the radical and back-to-nature advocate Scott Nearing. Old Helen was regaling us with all the cheery details of how she and Scott used to feed themselves, and among her handy tips was a recommendation that popcorn never be accompanied by butter and salt. Her reasoning had nothing to do with cholesterol or high blood pressure; the point she was making was that butter and salt would make the popcorn *taste too good*, thereby causing you to eat it with greater gusto and perhaps in greater volume than she thought appropriate. In other words, it would give you pleasure, and not merely stoke your fire. But Mrs. N. didn't stop there. She went on to point out that bread was a scarce commodity in her household, as she and Scott had come to realize that baking was an elaborate extravagance and that the same nutritive benefit could be obtained from chewing on raw wheat berries. The two of them must have had teeth like granary rats. We could go on, telling about how the Nearings shied away from honey because they felt that apiculture exploited the bees, but why should we torment you with such flapdoodle?

Helen and Scott Nearing are counterculture icons, and it has been the counterculture that has done a good deal of the proscriptive dietary yammering over the past twenty-five years. The word "radical," remember, comes from the Latin "radish," meaning "hot peppery root vegetable that you put next to celery to make Yankee antipasto." Anyway, part of the radical program for getting at the root of all that ailed Western society—all the things that led to racism, environmental depredation, the Vietnam War, and pro football—was to turn our eating habits upside down. It meant brown rice, adzuki beans, loaves of bread that could anchor a tugboat, meatless chili, tea made out of crabgrass, and a host of other comestibles and near-comestibles whose principal attraction (along with the fact that many of them came from the mysterious East, where people *really* have it together) was that they were not what straight people were eating. Carob, for instance, was a hot item because it was not chocolate. A lot of counterculturists would have walked backwards and eaten rocks if they could have gotten away with it.

Another aspect of the hip diet plan was to come down hard against extravagance, against the gilded lily syndrome that characterizes Western—and especially French—cuisine at its best. Unlike carob and adzuki beans, this idea struck a chord with society at large, as it tied in with our ancient Puritan strain as exemplified by the Baptist parents of old girlfriends. Somewhere around the late sixties or early seventies, you started to see newspaper food columns and with-it cookbooks using the soon-to-be-hackneyed line about "avoiding the use of heavy sauces that mask the flavors of the ingredients." This was part of the opening barrage of "Litespeak" that plagues us still, and it does some masking of its own: The truth is that the great tradition of sauces, heavy and otherwise, was created to supply us with dishes that were greater than the sum of their parts. But the new dictum answered that ancient urge for self-denial, as did paper-thin slices of duck breast arranged like flower petals.

Here's where the counterculture was joined by its old enemy, the bourgeoisie, in attacking the noble edifice of Good Eats. Somewhere along the line, the very elements of society that had once been obsessed with conspicuous consumption became obsessed with conspicuous *non*consumption. Of food, that is. We became a nation, as the restaurant consultant Clark Wolf has observed, in which "the best-educated, most affluent people . . . want to pay top-dollar to eat a third-world diet." Wolf was talking specifically about the current penchant for avoiding protein and fats, those two First World standbys, but his comment applies just as well to the simple volume of food people eat, and its inverse relationship to the tab at fashionable restaurants. What it all comes down to, as much as the desire to keep a little extra padding off one's keister, is the all-important element of *control*. Today's upscale mentality is one in which control is a major badge of accomplishment, and its one obvious manifestation—the appearance of having undertaken a deliberate program of undernourishment—is a way to lord it over all the poor, out-of-control putzes who don't need suspenders to hold up their pants.

The subject of control came up a while back, when one of us appeared on the *To Tell the Truth* TV show in connection with our last book, *Manifold Destiny* (the one about cooking on your car engine—go buy it). Each three-person team on the show consists of an individual who really is who he or she says they are, and two impostors; while we were all waiting for the taping to begin, a common pastime was to check out other teams and decide who was for real. One of the teams was assembled around a woman who had gotten herself off welfare and gone to Harvard Law School, and was now a hotshot attorney. A svelte little stockbroker with the superior air of the arch-yuppie was sitting at our end of the table, eyeing the three lawyer contestants. "It can't be the fat one," she said. "Nobody who looks like that could have the self-control to get through Harvard Law School." We told her that nobody as fat as Winston Churchill could get to be prime minister of Great Britain, either. She shot us a couple of daggers, but we had the last laugh when the fat lady turned out to be the lawyer.

Control, control. Ivana Trump came out with a good line not too long ago, one that sums up the whole neurotic preoccupation: "It makes me feel powerful to be hungry." There's a line Lillian Russell never used on Diamond Jim Brady.

Nowhere has the mania for demonstrating self-control as a display of one-upmanship gotten so silly—so out of control—as in the relationship between alcohol and its once-familiar terrain, the business world. Whenever you read articles full of tips for white-collar types these days, you invariably come across a warning against letting the demon rum cross your lips at a business lunch, particularly if you're being interviewed for a job or are playing power games with somebody (that about wraps up every conceivable business situation except for your retirement party, where you can get drunk and tell everybody to go pee up a rope). The message you'll put across, if you drink alcohol, is that you HAVE NO SELF-CONTROL. It's not that your colleagues will think you're a drunk. It's that they'll think you blinked in a crucial game of chicken, that you couldn't just say no, that you declared a measure of raffish independence tantamount to wearing a striped shirt at IBM in 1958.

Not that there isn't a very real trend toward neo-prohibitionism afoot in the land. *Esquire* magazine, that onetime bastion of worldliness, recently devoted one of its "Drinking Man" columns to Gatorade. This is the column where we first learned about straight rye whiskey! Well, we digress unnecessarily from the subject of food, but it's worth noting that the defeat of the Axis and the building of the most powerful economy the world has ever known were accomplished by guys who had a few snorts at lunch, while all the mineral water crowd has come up with are junk bonds and the sale of half the store to Japan.

For the yuppies, then, self-starvation—and denying oneself the chance to get properly sotted while some thundering bore ruins lunch by talking about spreadsheet software—is a matter of asserting control. For the politically correct, passing up the delights and superfluities of Western cuisine is a way of showing solidarity with the Third World, as if global hunger would somehow disappear if only the regularly fed would stop eating. There is a nail here that the late great gastronome Waverley Root hit squarely on the head in a *New York Times Magazine* article back in 1975. Root had written a piece on the decline of culinary taste, and was subsequently bombarded with letters from right-thinking readers who felt that gourmets ought to be extinct, in a world where people are starving. In his second article, Root asked why "so many egalitarian movements manage to end up advocating that the attempt to get everybody on the same footing should start by leveling down from the top instead of up from the bottom." Noting that the Puritan eats because "God has so organized the universe that he must"— preferably without talking about it—Root concludes his defense brilliantly: "As for the ill-fed," he wonders, "from whom may they expect the most sympathy—from those who like to eat or from those who don't?"

We see some hands up in the back row, and we know what you want to ask. What about the indisputable facts concerning diet and health? First of all, the only truly indisputable fact is that the *New England Journal of Medicine* comes out every week, and they have to put something in it. But if you want a serious answer (boy, are you reading the wrong book), let's backtrack to Puritanism, a dead horse we enjoy beating even more than egg yolks. Specifically, let's talk about the notion that a fall goeth after pride, or pleasure. It has to, to the Puritan, or life just doesn't make sense. Now, we are serious environmentalists—we recycle our lard boxes—but we have been wondering lately about the mentality that argues that every step taken in the direction of technological advancement must needs lead to a pie in the collective human face. There was a great example of this attitude a couple of years back, when those two nutty professors in Utah had the world thinking they had perfected fusion-in-a-jar. No sooner had the word gotten out that we might have finally tapped a cheap, clean, inexhaustible source of energy than several environmentalist writers started bemoaning the very idea of such a thing. Their reasoning was that if energy was free, we'd start wasting everything else. They felt that if we'd beaten the energy rap, we were being cheated out of our punishment for being nasty, acquisitive humans. Normal, mentally healthy people know that the main reason we're on earth, as individuals and as a species, is to figure out ways to eat our cake and still have it. This concept drives Puritans crazy; for the environmentalist of a Puritanical bent, it means that cheap, clean, boundless energy would ruin the sweaty little scenario of people pedaling stationary bicycles to run grist mills. Someday someone (probably not in Utah) will invent a nonpolluting Lincoln Town Car, and a great cry of anguish will go up from those who feel that every idle pleasure should be followed by a smack in the head.

You can easily see what all this has to do with food (if you can't, just skip ahead to the easier recipes, and don't hurt yourself with the potato peeler). The Puritan *wants* to find out that the stuff he enjoys eating is going to kill him, or at least keep him from being chaste in thought. The idea of retribution even predates the health industry's preoccupation with buggering up our diets—for how long, now, have we had to put up with ''sinful'' as a dessert cliché? That should have been a tipoff. In an increasingly secular age, when fewer and fewer people actually believe that committing ''sins'' is going to park their asses in "Hell," the notion of punishment seeks secular expression: eat that, and you're in for a bypass. (Interestingly, people who really do believe in sins and hell are more likely to run gut-busting church suppers.)

Those lucky souls who have not been afflicted by John Calvin and company know that it's actually the other way around: you don't seek out punishment to atone for pleasure; you seek out pleasure because life is already hard enough. Brillat-Savarin said it beautifully in *The Physiology of Taste*: "Man is, incontestably, among the sentient creatures who inhabit the globe, the one who endures the most pain . . . [this makes him] throw himself, without even realizing it, toward the opposite extreme, and give himself completely to the small number of pleasures which nature has permitted him." As anti-Puritans and staunch free-will advocates, we'll go the great Frenchman one better: if it's Wednesday and you still haven't felt any pain all week, make yourself a big rich dinner anyway.

It is the idea of punishment as an inescapable constant, meant for everyone, that lurks behind all the scares, fads, and dire warnings that make people look at their lunch as if it were a loaded gun. Essentially, there are two reasons why the gloomy voices in the media are telling you not to eat, or at least not to eat anything good: you might get fat (nowadays this means you won't be skinny), and you might have a heart attack. Everything else is a minor concern. Now, you can tell that you are getting fat if your pants don't fit. If they do fit (and for God's sake, do yourself a favor and buy them big enough in the first place), you are not getting fat. Relax and have two slices of our Pork Cake, page 139. As for heart attacks, these are a trickier business. We are not going to make any hard-and-fast recommendations here because we are not doctors and—far more important—we are not lawyers. But we know you can have your cholesterol level checked, along with your high-density lipids, low-density lipids, lipstick density, and aphids. The numbers often bear no relationship whatsoever to your diet. We know lanky triathlon types who are pushing 300, and sybaritic tubs gliding along at half that. The moral of the story is that you should be careful picking your grandfather. But the Food Police don't want to hear that. They want risk to be spread out democratically, even though life, as Jimmy Carter once said, is unfair. So everybody gets put on the same rations. It's as if you're being told to live on Uneeda biscuits and milk because the guy next door might get an ulcer. What we're saying is to read the numbers every so often, and if you ain't broke, don't fix yourself.

What you can fix is your diet. This little book is our way of getting you, who are healthy to begin with, reacquainted with some of the tasty things you may have been missing if you've been listening to the Legions of Lite. But *Bad-for-You* is good for you in more ways than one. What we have aimed for here is not just a collection of recipes, but a collection with a theme. We know, lots of cookbooks have themes. But the theme of most of them is that all the recipes come from northwest Turkey, or are made with lemons, or can be put together by a chimpanzee with a microwave oven, or some such arcane gimmick. Our theme is far more encompassing; our purpose is nothing less than to remind you what food was like when people ate either because they were hungry, or wanted to have a real good time, or both—not because they wanted to make a statement about how little they could get by on, or wanted to sample the latest designer cuisines, or wanted to put together restaurant menus studded with so many little Heart Association symbols that they look like Valentines for mice. There was a time when people were delightfully unself-conscious about what they ate, a time before the triumph of effete urban squeamishness, a time when everybody in the village turned out for hog-butchering day like in the movie *The Tree of Wooden Clogs*, with nary a citizen handing out pamphlets on behalf of the pig. It was a time when few people other than Sylvester Graham and John Harvey Kellogg ran the risk of developing nervous dyspepsia by worrying over every forkful that entered their maws; and *Bad for You* is our attempt to bring that time back for another hearty run.

Henry Aldrich once wrote a little verse succinctly explaining the reasons for drinking, one that might apply just as easily to eating. (Actually, the poem can be made to apply to a lot of things; we found it in N. Rayner and K. Chivers's *The Heavy Horse Manual,* as part of an explanation of why someone would want to own a Percheron. Poets are a serviceable lot.) It goes like this:

> *If all be true that I do think*
> *There are five reasons we should drink:*
> *Good wine—a friend—or being dry—*
> *Or lest we should be, by and by—*
> *Or any other reason why.*

Mangia!

CHAPTER 1

PIE
FOR
BREAKFAST

"I hope there's pie for breakfast, neighbor Stone."

THE WORDS WERE Daniel Webster's, spoken near the end of Stephen Vincent Benét's story "The Devil and Daniel Webster." Dan'l had just spent the night arguing with the forces of perdition, and that's hungry work. Since most of us spend our *days* arguing with the forces of perdition, we're just as much in need of sustenance at the breakfast hour.

You could do worse than pie. We've always had a strong mental image of the kind of pie that the newly reprieved Jabez Stone had in his buttery, and how it'd be served to the great lawyer. We picture an apple pie, its crust light and flaky as only lard can make it, the filling dense with moist slices of Greening or more likely some now-forgotten variety of apple that survives only in the gnarly brambles that crowd the abandoned cellarholes of upcountry New England. The pie is a day old and the crust and filling have settled; pies aren't a presentation piece in Jabez Stone's New Hampshire but just something you have around in varying states of wholeness. This one is half gone from yesterday's lunch, and Daniel Webster will soon make the other half gone, too.

Jabez Stone—or more likely Mrs. Stone, this being the early nineteenth century—will put that pie on a plate and then go back into the buttery to quarry off a slab of farm cheddar the size of a roofing slate. The cheese will lie atop the pie, and Daniel Webster will be happy. He'll wash it all down with a quart of hard cider, and then be off to a day of doing things people still remember, none the worse for not having broken his fast with three ounces of low-fat yogurt and an eyedropperful of decaffeinated coffee.

There, you've got one foolproof breakfast recipe already. Here are a few more, all of them fit to serve someone who's been up all night saving you from the clutches of the devil.

● ●

SCRAPPLE

Our first taste of scrapple came in the spring of 1983, in a down-at-the-heels lunch counter in a grimy market on Spring Green Street in Philadelphia. If this place had been in New York City, it would have been a bodega fringed by junkies. We, however, were the junkies—pork fat junkies. Our breakfast companion was also at heel level, a rummy hanger-on from one of the rowing clubs a few blocks away. His culinary contribution to the bleached world of racing shells was rigging the soda machine in his club to dispense Schlitz.

Ignoring the greasy scrambled eggs, we dug in. It was all we had hoped for, crispy on the outside and slightly creamy inside the way cornmeal can get after being simmered in stock for ages and then blasted with a high pressure front of sizzling fat. It had what appeared to be tiny hairs strewn within, leading us to believe we might be communing with Mr. Pig a little more closely than even we might wish. The threads, however, turned out to be meat fibers, the scrapple was sublime, and we wound up frequent visitors to Philadelphia.

Most scrapple recipes call for bulk sausage meat. Given that the epicenter of scrapple consumption is somewhat north of Boathouse Row, we prefer to go back to the origins of this humble pâté. If you can deal with wrestling the Holy Hog into a huge cauldron, you can drop lines like "No, nothing much is happening. I'm just boiling down a pig's head."

After a while it's like having a really fat-headed friend in the kitchen with you. Just stroll over, lift the lid, and gaze into the blank smile of Lester the Pig, your selfless benefactor. Doing his duty, he'll smile back.

1 medium pig's head, about 15 pounds, cleaned
  yellow cornmeal
  salt
  pepper
  sage or poultry seasoning
  flour for dredging
  fat for frying

- Put pig's head in large pot, cover with cold water, and cook at slow boil until meat falls off the bone. Cool and mince meat. Strain and degrease cooking liquid and bring to boil. Weigh meat; for every 3 pounds pork add 2 pounds meal to liquid. Cook to a mush. Add meat. For every pound pork add 1½ teaspoons salt, ½ teaspoon pepper, and 1 teaspoon sage or poultry seasoning. Cook slowly another half hour, stirring constantly, until mixture thickens. Pour into loaf pans and chill. Cut into ½-inch slices, dredge in flour, and fry until crispy.

• •

DOUGHNUTS
(À LA POMMES DE TERRE)

One of our favorite books while growing up was a volume of great schemes on how to get rich without really breaking a sweat, purchased by a father who was morally opposed to breaking one. A standout chapter detailed the growth of the Spudnut chain of doughnut shops. Spudnuts were, naturally, based on potatoes; even in our youth we knew this was a concept on which to ride rainbows.

Victims of deprived childhoods, we never did get a Spudnut. About twenty-five years later, in Bath, Maine, we inquired of a local where we might find a copy of the day's New York Times. *"Try the drugstore," a gentleman suggested. "It's right next to the Spudnut shop." We studiously avoided the temptation to leap from the car and smother the man with kisses; instead, we rammed the shift lever into first and snapped the clutch. We missed his toes.*

We were Galahad glimpsing the Grail in some infidel's hut; we were Ponce De Leon feeling our dowser's rod making a beeline for the magma. Here we were on the banks of the Kennebec, about to bear witness.

You may have guessed the ending. The Kennebec is in Maine, where anything you put up stays there until it either blows down or someone figures out a way to make soap or a snowmobile part out of it. Our gentleman's memories had not yet emulsified into Ivory. No one in the rather prosaic pastry shop had ever heard of Spudnuts; we got that nervous feeling that twitches up when we realize that the English language is only a very extended metaphor and that once in a while we all reach into the wrong drawer.

So, when you try this recipe, try to serve them across a countertop of Formica. Try to be sitting next to a woman wearing her hair in a bun. Hope that she's wearing a hairnet.

  1 cup hot mashed potatoes
  2 tablespoons butter
  2 eggs
 ⅔ cup sugar
  2 cups flour
  2 teaspoons baking powder
1½ teaspoons salt
    generous grating of nutmeg
    fat for deep frying

- Put hot potatoes in mixing bowl with butter; stir until butter is melted and mixed in. Let mixture cool. Mix in eggs; sift dry ingredients together into mixture and stir until smooth.
- On floured surface, with well-floured rolling pin, roll dough to ½ inch. Using floured doughnut cutter, punch out doughnuts. Gather scraps together and repeat until dough is used up. Fry a few at a time in deep fat at 360°. Turn carefully with slotted spoon when they rise to surface. Continue turning and frying until well browned. Drain on paper towels. Eat while still hot.

THE HOTEL BREAKFAST
OF OUR DREAMS

When we think of the truly grand hotels, our reveries turn not to such things as indoor pools, all-night health spas, and bathrooms with computer modems, nor even to such traditional luxuries as the heated towel racks at the Cipriani in Venice or the wood-burning fireplaces at the Boston Ritz-Carlton. No, we think of breakfast, and of the delights peculiar to breakfast menus at old-fashioned, first-rate hotels. We thought it would be fun to conjure up a Dream Hotel Breakfast for Two, and send our readers out to find it. Even if it eludes you, it's something to fantasize as you pick over your room service "Businessperson's Rise 'n' Shine," consisting of a cup of luke-warm coffee, a leather croissant, and a copy of *USA Today*.

Room service, of course.

We're conjuring a breakfast ferried up to your room along with all the accoutrements you'd find in the dining room—starched linen, flowers, incredibly heavy silver covered with the little hairline scratches that come from having been washed several times each day since 1928. And, of course, it's a Sunday morning. Here's the menu:

Fresh-squeezed Orange Juice
Kadota Figs in Heavy Syrup
Sliced Bananas with Heavy Cream
Finnan Haddie
Roast Beef Hash with Poached Eggs
Creamed Hashed Brown Potatoes
Toast, with Butter and Marmalade
Fresh Blueberry Muffins
Coffee, in an enormous silver pot

For reading material, we'd like *The New York Times,* along with two freshly sharpened pencils for the puzzle, and the best local paper—something with the funnies. If the *Times* carried the funnies, the world would be too nice to live in.

8

EGG-FILLED CORNED BEEF RING

Although we've had more than our share (more than our share seems to be an underlying theme here) of wonderful homemade corned beef hash, we prefer the canned version for this dish. Perhaps it's the creamy texture resulting from over-processing, or maybe that Hormel is willing to dose the hash with more fat than even we might, but the canned stuff develops a better crispy-shell-to-molten-innards ratio.

Obviously, we've gone to great lengths to arrive at a delicate balance of flavors here, so don't be a Philistine and reach for the catsup.

3　15-ounce cans corned beef hash
6　tablespoons butter
6　tablespoons flour
1　cup milk
1　cup heavy cream
2　tablespoons tomato paste
　　salt and pepper
8　eggs

- Spoon hash into greased 12-inch ring mold and place in 375° oven for about 30 minutes or until bubbling at edges and browned on top.
- Meanwhile, make sauce: melt butter in saucepan and when foam subsides add the flour; stir to mix well and cook over medium heat a minute or two, stirring constantly. Bring milk and cream to boiling and whisk into roux. Cook a few minutes, breaking up any lumps. Add tomato paste and salt and pepper and cook until slightly thickened.
- Poach the eggs, leaving yolks liquid. Trim uneven edges to make neat ovals. Unmold hash onto serving platter. Carefully arrange eggs in center of ring and pour sauce over all.

● ●

KEDGEREE

If you want to understand why the pew cushions in New England white-steepled churches are so thin, make a batch of kedgeree. If you're wondering why some of them don't even have cushions, make it without the butter and milk.

Every time we've made this, we've had visions of wispy-haired Maine farmers huddled near a low fire. The cows have been milked, but the clapboards on the farmhouse are loose and the wind sneaks in. It's cold as hell and a schooner is busy washing up on the rocks a few miles away. It's nearing the end of February and the potatoes are getting a little wormy, so it's time to sift the mealybugs out of the rice and eat up the remains of last night's boiled fish, then go off to church for the day.

Enjoy.

1   cup raw white rice
2   tablespoons butter
4   hard-boiled eggs
2   cups cooked fish (haddock, cod, or any firm-fleshed white fish), broken into large flakes
½   cup milk or cream
    salt and pepper

- Put rice, 2 cups water, and butter in small saucepan. Bring to boil, stir, cover and cook until all water is absorbed, about 17 minutes. When done, turn into mixing bowl and fluff.
- Chop the eggs and add to rice along with fish, milk or cream, and salt and pepper. Mix very well; heat in double boiler until steaming.

●   ●

FINNAN HADDIE

Finnan Haddie, a salted fish, doesn't always hit it off with every diner on the first date. Our first taste came in a small bed and breakfast in London, and it confirmed all our prejudices about the way the Brits pretend to cook. Luckily, one of us had the good taste to cover it with thickened milk and melted cheese, and it suddenly got a lot better. Naturally, it was the one without any English ancestors. The preferred serving arrangement consists of oven-fried potatoes surrounding the fish, sticking upright to resemble those trees Macbeth saw off in the distance.

- 1 pound finnan haddie
- 2 cups milk
- 3 tablespoons butter
- 3 tablespoons flour
- ½ cup grated semi-hard cheese (Gruyère, swiss, provolone, etc.)

- In a large saucepan, cover fish with milk, bring to simmer, and poach until flesh flakes easily. Melt butter until foam subsides. Add flour and stir with spoon or whisk over medium heat for a few minutes to make a roux. Add milk from poaching pan and continue to cook, stirring, until nicely thickened.
- Butter a baking pan. Add fish, cover with sauce and sprinkle with cheese. Run under broiler until nicely browned.

CATCH OF THE DAY

CORNMEAL-AND-BACON-FAT BROOK TROUT

Here's one straight from Nick Adams's dream fields. Get up early enough to catch some dew-sopped grasshoppers and go down to the river long enough to haul in a few trout. Although the recipe calls for a 12-incher, the best ones are the little 5- to 8-inch babies. Because of various fish and game laws we don't want to encourage this sort of thing. Plus, it would be wrong.

Return to camp, stir up the fire, and get ready to eat. If you're like us you'll have packed in a couple of cast iron frying pans so you can fry the eggs as the trout sizzles.

> 1 freshly caught brook trout, about 12 inches long
> ½ cup milk
> 1 cup yellow cornmeal
> 5 slices bacon

- Scale and gut trout. Dip in milk and coat thoroughly in cornmeal.
- Fry bacon to desired crispness. Remove from pan and toss in trout. Cook a few minutes on each side, until bones lift away easily. Serve, with bacon slices on the side.

• •

EAST INDIAN SPAGHETTI BREAKFAST

Many years ago, we helped an East Indian family move from Vermont to Rhode Island. When we got there and started helping them unload their truck, we noticed two things: First, they had their household Gods in a cardboard box marked "Gods." The God box, they told us, was the first one you were supposed to open in your new house. The second thing we noticed was that the first box they opened was the one that said "Liquor." Such is the nature of assimilation into the West. Next morning, though, they served us a very unassimilated breakfast, which they assured us was traditional despite the substitution of spaghetti for native Indian noodles.

I hope the Gods forgave them.

    6 tablespoons olive oil
    I large onion, chopped
    2 cloves garlic, chopped
    I pound spaghetti, cooked al dente, rinsed in cold water,
          drained, and cooled completely
    ¾ cup shelled roasted peanuts
    ½ cup shredded coconut
    ½ teaspoon seeded chopped dried hot pepper
    ½ teaspoon turmeric
    I teaspoon curry powder
       salt and pepper

• Heat oil in a large frying pan (a wok will also do) and sauté onion and garlic until golden. Add cold spaghetti and toss. Add all remaining ingredients, tossing to mix well; if you wish, you may adjust the amounts of Indian spices to taste, or use your own mixture instead of premixed curry powder. Cumin and cardamom are interesting additions. Toss so all ingredients are thoroughly distributed, then let sit at medium heat so that a crust begins to form on spaghetti. Toss every so often, allowing crust to form in between tossings. When spaghetti is heated through and crusty bits are nicely distributed, serve.

• •

SHIRRED EGGS

When we were kids, we used to stay in an old-fashioned hotel every summer as part of a vacation jaunt around New England. One of the things we liked best about this dinosaur inn was the breakfast menu (see sidebar, page 8), which we took great delight in ordering from by reciting the exact phrase used to describe each dish we wanted: "I'd like the golden griddlecakes with pure creamery butter and Vermont maple syrup, and a rasher of bacon." Dad could have crawled under the table. Anyway, the one thing we never ordered, no matter how much we wanted to trip the name off our tongue, was shirred eggs. They sounded great, but we were suspicious as to just what the shirring process might involve. Years later when we found out that the secret ingredient was nothing other than heavy cream, we wanted to run back to the old hotel and tell the kitchen to shir us up a batch. We didn't, because the shirred eggs on the menu have now been replaced, we suspect, by a fruit plate with yogurt.

> butter
> 3 eggs
> 3 tablespoons heavy cream

• Butter individual ramekins (egg coddlers). Break eggs and carefully add 1 egg to each ramekin. Cover each with a tablespoon of cream. Bake at 350° about 20 minutes, or until white is set.

CHAPTER 2

MEAT
AND
POTATOES

THERE WAS AN item in *The New York Times* the other day about how to select the right cut of meat for pot roast. It's a sorry commentary on the age that the *Times* even had to run such a piece; not so long ago, people just grew up knowing how to make pot roast the way they knew how to shine their shoes. There's another simple art that's been lost, now that everybody wears white sneakers and polishes them with mud.

Anyway, the *Times* writer got to talking about larding, the old-fashioned process of taking long, thin pieces of fat and threading them through a piece of meat considered too lean to have the proper flavor and moistness once cooked. There's a utensil for this job, called a larding needle, which you may still find in kitchen equipment shops run by flagrant reactionaries. (It's fun to ask for it in trendy gourmet shops and watch people blanch.) "We used to lard the fat right through the meat," the article quotes a veteran New York butcher as saying. "Nobody asks for that anymore. All people want now is to see no fat and eat chicken, chicken, chicken. It's taken the fun part out."

Unfortunately, fat is being removed from meat at the genetic research level as well as in the butcher shop. We saw a comparison chart recently, which showed the silhouettes of typical hogs down through the last fifty years or so. It only took a little mental extrapolation for us to conclude that the main objective of hog research is to eventually produce swine with the contours of greyhounds, capable of entertaining the masses at pig tracks complete with pari-mutuel windows.

Things are a lot sunnier in the potato industry, probably

because carbohydrates are currently in favor. As you can see from the multitude of entrants in our potato taste test (page 37), agricultural science has given us a splendid array of potato varieties, and as far as we can tell none of them have been denied the essence of potatoness. Potatoes have come a long way from the original Peruvian varieties, little yellow and blue things that the Spanish conquistadors found in the course of shaking down the Inca empire for silver and gold.

Take up your larding needle and your potato peeler, then, and keep as your motto our paraphrase of Keats: Meat and potatoes are all ye know on earth, and all ye need to know.

The rest is gravy.

● ●

BISCUITS AND GRAVY

If the Oxford English Dictionary were to study the roots of the old phrase "sticks to your ribs," Louisville, Kentucky, might be a good place to start. It's always been a well-stocked hunting ground for our kind of food (it's so well stocked that it resembles those "hunting" resorts for the rich and shiftless where the animals are fenced in, guaranteeing the hunter whatever "trophy" might have been air-freighted in from Africa the week before). We've come up with a couple of good reasons for this.

After years of success on his own, Colonel Sanders was finally persuaded to sell out to a group headed by John Y. Brown. Later (not to imply cause and effect) Mr. Brown married the former Miss America, Phyllis George; the ceremony was performed by Norman Vincent Peale. The good minister's service was so inspiring that Mr. Brown decided he owed the world something; he ran and became governor of the State of Kentucky (definitely cause and effect). It follows that the state bird should be a well-fried chicken.

Secondly, Louisville is crisscrossed by so many different railroad lines that there's always a wrong side of the tracks handy, making a dandy environment for checking out dishes with "traditional values."

We first discovered biscuits and gravy in a cafeteria that turned into a bar after lunchtime. Simplicity itself, the plate has nothing more than two or three split biscuits covered by a ladleful of white sticky gravy studded here and there with tiny chunks of sausage meat. If you want you can put some butter on the biscuits but to us that's a bit of an uptown affectation. The whole thing shouldn't set you back more than a dollar.

Animal rights' activists should note that, according to the blues singer Albert King, if you make the biscuits extra big, they're known as "cats' heads." Ahem.

½ cup fat from frying sausage
½ cup flour
1 quart boiling water
   any pan juices from sausages (as opposed to more fat, or at least a lot more fat)
1 recipe Cream Biscuits (page 54)
   salt and pepper
½ cup well-fried, crumbled pork sausage

- In saucepan, heat fat until it starts to bubble slightly. Add flour, stir well, and cook for several minutes over medium heat. Do not allow to brown. Add boiling water and pan juices and let simmer until thickened, stirring frequently. Meanwhile, heat biscuits and arrange on plates. Add salt and pepper to taste, and fried sausage, to gravy, mix well, and pour over biscuits. Serve with butter on side for sissies. (Note: Experience will teach you the best biscuit/gravy ratio. On one hand, you don't want too few biscuits; on the other, you can't have too much gravy.)

● ●

YORKSHIRE PUDDING

Yorkshire pudding is a problem for us. At its best, it's cooked in the fat left in the pan after the roast has been removed. At its worst, it's a slop of insipid batter that somehow is frozen into the shape of the Pillsbury Doughboy's nightmares without ever cooking through. It reached its nadir in the early seventies when restaurants started priding themselves on the size of their popovers, which are nothing more than the same batter plopped into a muffin pan. In the twenties, Ernest Hemingway tried to convince a forlorn Scott Fitzgerald that size didn't matter; the same advice applies to blurs of leathery dough that look like tan baby shoes on steroids.

Probably the best thing Yorkshire pudding can do for us is to grab some sausages and make itself into Toad in the Hole (see next recipe).

  1 cup flour
  2 eggs, well beaten
  1 cup milk
     dash of salt
  4 tablespoons lard or fresh beef drippings (fat)

- Sift flour into bowl. Make a well in center and stir in the eggs and a couple of tablespoons of the milk, along with the salt. Mix with a fork, gradually mixing in flour from edge of well. When mixed, add remaining milk and stir well.
- Heat oven to 400°. Put fat in an 11-by-14-inch shallow baking dish and heat until very hot but not smoking. Pour batter into dish and return to oven and bake 30 to 40 minutes until puffed and browned.

● ●

TOAD IN THE HOLE

Imagine the world of cooking set down in the land of fairy tales. Pick a rather pale, fairly comatose dish like Yorkshire pudding and rename it Snow White. Now pick a well-rounded, upright food, say, just for the sake of argument, a fresh garlic sausage. Call it Prince Charming. Put them together and they're both transformed; sometimes adding A to B gives you C, and sometimes it gives you the whole alphabet.

Now that the European Common Market is going full tilt, the possibilities are unlimited for sausage-batter combinations. French chippolatas, German brats, small, fine-grained Italian salamis are all delighted to assume nesting places in the soft batter.

The question to ponder is, if you make it in the Cotswolds with French sausage, does it become Froggie in the Chunnel?

¼ cup lard or fresh beef drippings
1 pound fresh small pork sausages
1 batch Yorkshire Pudding batter (see above)

- Put fat in an 11-by-14-inch shallow baking dish. Put in 400° oven for a few minutes until fat is very hot but not smoking.
- Meanwhile, poach sausages in simmering water for 5 minutes. Prick well to release excess fat.
- Pour enough batter into baking dish to cover the bottom. Return to oven a few minutes to let batter set, then distribute sausages over pan and pour remaining batter over all. Bake 30 to 40 minutes, until puffed and brown.

● ●

ROAST BEEF WITH OVEN-BROWNED POTATOES

We admit this may cause some of the clean-oven movement to get antsy, but it's worth it (getting them antsy, that is). A couple of Christmas Eves ago we spit-roasted two chickens before an open fire. Partway through the roasting time, we propped a pan full of parboiled potatoes under the spit to catch both the drippings and the heat from the coals. Purists might claim that it was using an original fireplace from 1795 that gave us one of the ultimate batches of potatoes; being purists of another strain, we attributed the success to the drippings carpet-bombing the entire dish. However, few roasting pans have racks high enough to accommodate potatoes beneath them.

The easy, if ever so slightly messy, solution is to trade the roaster rack for the oven rack, with the potato dish strategically placed below the meat. Sure, the fat might splatter a bit, but having the tubers receive a constant bath in fat and pan juices makes all the difference in the world. If you plan on doing this frequently you might want to buy an oven like ours—the entire inside is jet black. We think it came that way.

> vegetable oil
> 5 - pound top loin of beef, rolled and tied
> 3 tablespoons butter
> ½ cup beef broth
> 3 pounds boiling potatoes

- Preheat oven to 425°. Rub top oven rack with oil. Rub ends of beef with oil. Place beef directly on oven rack. Beneath beef place large shallow roasting pan on lower rack. Put butter and broth in pan. Roast 15 minutes, then turn oven to 325°.

- Meanwhile, peel potatoes and quarter lengthwise. Parboil five minutes, drain well, and add to roasting pan when lowering temperature to 325°. Spread out evenly below beef.
- From time to time, baste beef with pan juices. At the same time, toss potatoes well with spoon or spatula. Roast about 1¼ to 1½ hours, or until meat thermometer reads 120° for rare, 125° for medium rare. If you're going to roast it longer, why bother?
- Serve with a béarnaise or Madeira sauce (see below).

·

BÉARNAISE SAUCE

  2 teaspoons finely chopped shallots
1½ teaspoons, plus generous pinch, tarragon
     salt and pepper
  5 tablespoons red wine vinegar
  5 egg yolks
12 tablespoons butter
⅛ teaspoon cayenne pepper, or less
  1 tablespoon minced parsley (optional)

- Combine shallots, 1½ teaspoons tarragon, salt and pepper to taste, and vinegar in small saucepan. Bring to boil and reduce until ⅓ of vinegar remains. Remove from heat, let cool slightly, and mix in the egg yolks. Return to low heat and whisk in the butter, tablespoon by tablespoon. Since this is nothing more than mayonnaise made with butter instead of oil, it will curdle if overheated, so use gentle heat. When all butter is incorporated into the sauce, force through a sieve, and add the pinch of tarragon, cayenne, and parsley, if desired.

·

MADEIRA SAUCE

    4 tablespoons butter
    4 tablespoons flour
 1½ cups beef stock (use canned bouillon if necessary)
   ½ cup good-quality red wine
    1 clove garlic, peeled
   ½ cup Madeira
    1 teaspoon fresh thyme
    2 tablespoons minced parsley
       salt and pepper

- In medium saucepan, melt butter until froth subsides. Add flour, mix well. Lower heat and cook, stirring constantly, for several minutes. In separate saucepan, bring beef stock and red wine to boil; add to roux along with garlic clove and continue to stir until sauce starts to thicken. Add Madeira and continue to simmer until sauce reaches desired thickness. Remove garlic clove; add thyme, parsley, and salt and pepper to taste.

● ●

ANYTHING CROQUETTES

The greatest natural enemy of the croquette has always been the steam table. Unnerved by memories of high school or the Army, many diners reflexively shy away from leftovers and their primary fate: high diving into a cream sauce, taking a quick shower in beaten eggs, somersaulting through the bread crumbs with a final, glorious back flip into hot sputtering fat.

We firmly believe in eating our croquettes the same day we make them (no reheating), and serving them with something equally earth-toned, usually mashed potatoes or hot buttered egg noodles.

  2　tablespoons butter
  3　tablespoons flour
1¼　cups milk, heated to boiling
  2　cups finely chopped anything already cooked (chicken, fish,
　　　ham, pork, beef, veal, canned tuna, potatoes, chopped
　　　onions, braised celery, green beans, mushrooms, etc.)
　　salt and pepper
  1　teaspoon appropriate spices (rosemary with chicken or
　　　pork, thyme with mushrooms, etc.)
  2　eggs, beaten
  2　cups fine fresh bread crumbs
　　fat for deep-frying

- Melt butter in saucepan. When foam subsides, add flour and stir with whisk or wooden spoon. Cook a few minutes until flour loses its raw smell. Add the milk in thin stream, stirring to eliminate lumps. Cook a few minutes until thickened. Pour into mixing bowl and cool.
- Add chopped anything, stirring to distribute evenly. Add salt and pepper and appropriate spices and mix well. Refrigerate for 2 hours.
- Form mixture with hands into any shape you wish, although tradition seems to dictate either cork-shaped croquettes or those in the shape of truncated cones. Two cups of filling will make 8 croquettes.
- Dip croquettes in beaten egg to coat, then dip in bread crumbs, making sure to cover all surfaces. Let dry on waxed paper or foil for about a half hour, then fry in 360° fat until brown.

● ●

CHRIS AND BILL GO CAMPING: THE CONTENTS OF THE DULUTH

In July of 1984, we loaded a sixteen-foot canoe onto the baggage car of a passenger train in Montreal, parked ourselves in the lounge car, and had ourselves dropped off at a point in the Ontario wilderness some eight hundred miles away. The idea was to follow a mapped canoe route for sixty miles to a little town elsewhere on the railroad line, pick up the train, and head back to civilization. The canoeing part worked out fine, despite the best efforts of mosquitos and badly marked portages to bugger it up (as they say in Canada). But the reason we're telling you about it has less to do with the paddle than the pan—the cast iron pan, to be exact, and the things we put in it over the course of six days. A lot of people think that wilderness experiences have to involve freeze-dried stew and gorp, but we're here to tell you otherwise. On our trip, we ate like the guys who brought back the beaver pelts that built Montreal, and the guys who hacked out a path for the Canadian Pacific Railway. We'll match their backwoods know-how against the powdered-egg crowd any day.

The essential carryall for canoe portaging is called a "Duluth," and it looks like Arnold Schwarzenegger's Boy Scout pack. It has a single compartment and a pair of shoulder straps—nothing fancy or highly engineered, since the figuring is that you'll only be carrying it on portages (none of ours were more than a mile), and the rest of the time it will just sit in the canoe. When it came time to plan our larder, our thinking went like this: The canoe will be no harder to paddle with a little more weight amidships. The portages will involve a lot of cursing, sweating, and mosquito bites, regardless of whether the Duluth weighs 50 pounds or 75. And we will be hungry almost all of the time. So, in addition to the all-important 10-inch cast iron pan (supplement to two ancient Boy Scout cooking kits), here's what we brought:

1 pound lard
1 pound butter
2 pounds slab bacon

2 pounds flour (some plain; some mixed with ingredients for
pancakes)
1 pound elbow macaroni
2 pounds Vermont cheddar
Powdered milk
Sugar
Honey
1 pound coffee
Tea bags
1 dozen eggs, in crush-resistant plastic "egg suitcase"
10 potatoes
2 pounds carrots
2 pounds onions
2 heads garlic
3 lemons
2 loaves unsliced dark rye bread
1 pound smoked summer sausage
3 pounds chocolate bars, semi-sweet with almonds
1 pound peanut butter
1 pound strawberry jam
Assorted spices
2 New York strip steaks (frozen in Montreal, for dinner on the
first night off the train)
7 bottles wine
1 quart bourbon
1 quart calvados
1 quart cognac

(Keep in mind that the last four items were for dinner and
campfire time only; friends don't let friends paddle drunk.) Needless
to say, we fared sumptuously. Except for the steak on the first night
out, and one night of macaroni and cheese (to the noodles and
cheddar listed above, we added a béchamel made on the spot), we
dined on fresh pickerel every night; the wines had been selected
accordingly. We never regretted a single ounce; in fact, there are a
few things we might add if we did it again. Maybe a box of Havana
Upmanns; they sell them in Montreal.

●

POTATOES FRIED IN GOOSE FAT

Goose fat and Idaho potatoes seem to be one of the holier alliances, ranking with tomatoes and basil, or olive oil and garlic. Perhaps it's significant that, if you're both nearsighted and color blind, an Idaho and a goose egg look alike.

In one of her earlier cookbooks, Julia Child has a recipe for "Ragoût d'oie au chou," goose pieces braised with cabbage. Besides yielding a marvelous dinner, the goose contains so much interior fat that, after rendering, there's enough to keep your table groaning with fried potatoes for many happy meals. One of the lessons here is that when you see the direction "Fry," your first question should be "In what?". And we don't mean frying pans.

> large amount of Idaho potatoes
> smaller, but not insignificant amount of rendered goose fat
>   (see note on rendering, page 115)
> salt and pepper

- Peel potatoes and cut in ¼-inch slices. Melt the goose fat in the largest skillet available and add potatoes. Cook over medium-high heat until golden brown on outside and very creamy on inside. Sprinkle with salt and pepper. Butter is not needed.

● ●

SOUTHERN SALT-PORK-POTATO-ONION-CRACKER-CHICKEN-FLOUR-PASTE PIE

Sometimes we run short of words. This one-dish meal empties your larder and hauls your ashes.

½ pound salt pork
 3 large yellow onions
 4 pounds boiling potatoes
 2 stewing hens
 1 quart oyster crackers, large if possible
 2 cups milk
 1 cup melted butter or bacon drippings
 4 cups flour
1½ teaspoons thyme
 ½ cup minced parsley
    salt and pepper
 2 tablespoons butter
 ½ teaspoon powdered cloves
 ½ bottle white wine

- Slice salt pork as thinly as possible. Slice onions thinly, and potatoes into ¼-inch slices. Cut chickens into serving pieces. Soak crackers in milk. Make a paste by stirring the melted fat into the flour, then working in enough water to make a thick, dough-like paste. Roll out into several sheets the size of your baking pan.

- Place some of the pork slices in the bottom of a Dutch oven. Add some of the onions, potatoes, soaked crackers, and a layer of chicken pieces. Sprinkle with some of the thyme, parsley, and salt and pepper. Cover with a layer of paste; repeat layers until oven is filled, finishing with the flour paste.

- Cut a vent hole in center and slowly pour in hot water until ¼ inch below top crust. Dot with butter, sprinkle with cloves, and add white wine. Place, covered, in 275° oven until just a bit of gravy remains, about 4 hours.

●   ●

BIG CHICKEN PIE

As we pointed out in our last cookbook, Bill and Chris are separate entities who live in separate houses and eat off plates with different patterns. The royal we aside, we each have a mother and father, and, correspondingly, each has two male and female grandparents. So, when we speak of our grandmother's recipe, it's anyone's guess which grandmother we're talking about. Simple enough?

This bulletproof chicken pie was one of the set pieces for large family dinners at our grandmother's. The last time we made it the contents of the finished product weighed in at 11½ pounds, which, interestingly enough, was the birthweight of one of our nephews.

Guess which sister.

     1 stewing chicken, about 6 to 8 pounds
        salt and pepper
     8 medium carrots, peeled
     4 medium onions, peeled
    12 medium-small boiling potatoes, about 2 pounds
    ¾ cup butter
     4 ribs celery (optional)
    ½ cup flour
     2 cups cream or half-and-half
     1 recipe Flaky Piecrust Dough (see page 32)

- Place chicken in large pot with water to cover, adding salt and pepper, 2 carrots, and 1 onion. Bring to boil, then simmer, partially covered, for about 2 hours, or until tender. Skim foam as it forms on surface. Remove from heat and let chicken cool in liquid. Remove chicken and reduce stock to 5 cups. Set stock aside to cool.

- Put potatoes in salted water to cover and parboil, cooking about 15 minutes after reaching boil. Put remaining 6 carrots in another pot with salted water to cover and cook about 10 minutes after reaching boil.
- Chop remaining 3 onions and sauté lightly in ¼ cup of the butter. If using celery, chop and sauté along with onions.
- Slice cooked potatoes in half lengthwise, then in ⅜-inch slices. Cut carrots into ½-inch slices. Remove meat from chicken and cut in bite-size pieces (don't forget all the little tidbits). Save wishbone for dire need.
- Make a roux: melt remaining ½ cup butter in large saucepan. When foam subsides, add flour and cook over medium heat until very lightly browned and raw flour smell is gone. Meanwhile, mix stock with cream and bring to boil. Add boiling liquid to roux and stir with whisk or wooden spoon to eliminate lumps. Cook at gentle boil until nicely thickened. Remove from heat; add chicken and vegetables and mix well. Correct seasonings.
- Drape larger piece of rolled crust over 11-by-14-inch baking dish. Gently press dough into corners and sides, leaving at least ½-inch overhang along edges. Prick bottom all over with fork and place in 425° oven for 10 minutes. Remove and fill with chicken/vegetable/sauce mixture. Cover with remaining dough, sealing at edges. Cut vent holes in top crust and bake at 425° for 10 minutes, then at 350° for 40 minutes, or until crust is lightly browned and pie is bubbling at edges and through vent holes. Let sit for 15 minutes before serving. No side dishes necessary.

·

FLAKY PIECRUST DOUGH

4 cups flour
6 teaspoons baking powder
1 teaspoon baking soda
1½ tablespoons sugar
2 teaspoons salt
1⅓ cups chilled shortening (½ butter and ½ solid vegetable shortening or lard)
2 cups milk, more or less

- Combine dry ingredients in mixing bowl. Cut in shortening with pastry cutter. Add enough milk to make a soft biscuit dough.
- Divide dough into 2 pieces, about 40 percent and 60 percent. On floured surface, gently roll out larger piece to line baking pan. When pan is filled with chicken mixture, roll out smaller piece to form top crust.

CHICKEN PUDDING

An old recipe from Virginia, chicken pudding illustrates the value in knowing various cooking methods. Cooks of the eighteenth and early nineteenth centuries took an almost perverse (although often dictated by necessity) pleasure in how many different versions they could produce of one dish. It's almost like God cranking out all the peoples of the earth and wondering how many different kinds He can get by twisting the mold. For variety, puddings beat even hash. As for perversity, pudding with bones in it is one twisted mold.

    4 frying chickens
    ½ cup butter
    4 ribs celery, chopped
    I medium onion, peeled and chopped
    6 eggs
    I quart milk
    2 cups flour
       salt and pepper

- Cut the chickens into serving pieces, reserving the giblets. Melt half the butter in a large skillet and slowly cook the chicken and celery, covered tightly, until tender. Turn pieces frequently. When done remove with slotted spoon, saving any cooking liquids. Meanwhile, simmer giblets in saucepan with the onion and water to cover. When done, set aside to cool.
- Melt remaining butter and mix with eggs, milk, and flour to form a batter, adding generous amounts of salt and pepper. Stir well to eliminate lumps. Put chicken pieces in deep baking dish and cover with batter. Bake in 350° oven about 45 minutes, or until nicely browned.
- Mince giblets and add to cooking liquids from chickens. Thicken if needed, using a paste of equal parts butter and flour. If there is not enough gravy, extend with hot stock.

● ●

PERFECT MASHED POTATOES

An honored guest at our family's Thanksgiving table for the past forty years has been the Penguin, a rotund, shining product of the West Bend Aluminum Company, Patent number 2,349,099. An insulated serving dish, it was generally available for about one dollar at yard sales until "design consciousness" forced yuppies to buy it. The godfather of hip must like those eight little embossed penguins marching around the dish's equator because the price has skyrocketed.

For all its charms, there is one thing the Penguin cannot do and that is keep mashed potatoes in a proper state; for forty years our mother has always given it one more chance. While we've always admired fortitude, we wish she'd realize that there is no way to keep potatoes hot and maintain the proper texture. Time your cooking so that you serve them no more than 5 minutes after the butter melts. Eat them, enjoy them, but don't put the lid on them.

If you want good seconds, serve them with your firsts.

  6 baking potatoes (also known as Idaho or russet)
  8 tablespoons butter
  ½ cup hot milk
     salt and pepper

- Peel and quarter the potatoes. Place in saucepan with salted water to cover and boil, covered, until tender when pierced with knife. Drain and return to pan, shaking briefly over medium heat to evaporate excess water.
- Add 6 tablespoons of the butter and hot milk. Mash thoroughly. Add salt and lots of black pepper. Do not whip. Do not beat. When butter is melted and milk is well mixed, stir once with wooden spoon and turn into serving bowl. Garnish with 2 remaining tablespoons butter.

• •

Caveat: There are various methods of reheating mashed potatoes before serving; none of them work. The only acceptable way of reheating them is to form into cakes and fry in butter. However, they then become potato cakes, not mashed potatoes. Given the glories of the potato, timing your dinner properly is not too much to ask.

TUBER TOONS, or
Fun Things to Know About Spuds

In 1586 Sir Francis Drake gave a mature potato plant to Queen Elizabeth, who handed it over to her cook, who, besides being a British cook, had never seen a potato before. He stripped off the leaves and cooked them, throwing away the rest. The Queen didn't like them. Closer to home, Anna Thomas, author of the cloying *The Vegetarian Epicure* ("a book about joy") wondered in 1972 what to do with raw leftover potatoes, denuded to make "potato peel broth."

She should have picked up *Larousse Gastronomique;* it lists ninety-nine potato recipes. Or maybe she didn't have a copy of *The Escoffier Cook Book* handy, which gives sixty-one ways to make the once-lowly tuber. Personally, we would have asked her to shut up and fry them in lots of hot lard.

The potato was cultivated as far back as 2,000 B.C., at altitudes up to 15,000 feet. Spanish explorers brought them back from South America, along with the Incas' gold. Europeans didn't really have much to do with them for a couple of centuries; at one point a French provincial department banned them as a source of leprosy. Finally, in 1771 Parmentier presented his famous thesis and modern spud cuisine began.

Being 77 percent water, potatoes have been a staple of poorer cultures and the bane of rich dieters. We've always enjoyed pointing out to neurotic thin people that with 90 calories, a potato comes in 27 calories under an apple. Besides, whoever heard of apples Anna, or French-fried apples, or mashed apples with garlic? Potatoes have enough vitamin C to prevent scurvy and are a good source of potassium; they're the only vegetable to get their own chapter in James Beard's *American Cookery*.

Members of the same plant family as tomatoes (that's why they rhyme), they at times shared the stigma of being thought poisonous. Although there have been a few cases of toxic doses of alkaloids from grossly mishandled tubers, we've never paid heed to Mrs. Rorer, who at the turn of the century damned potato water as "unsafe for food" or another writer who said it was "known to poison a dog." The main deaths attributed to potatoes were the 1,000,000 Irish in the famine of 1845–1849, and those came from *not* eating them.

With the proliferation of "couch potatoes," spuds are making a comeback. Trendy restaurants in sinkholes like New York City are dropping the tuna carpaccio and serving mashers along with expensive meat loaf. We're all for it, although we think Julia Child, in *The Way To Cook,* plays a bit to the cheap seats when she declares that instant potatoes "can be remarkably good."

In the interest of science, we decided to do a technically rigid taste test.

Taking a deep breath, we plunged into that paragon of excess, Dean and DeLuca, a gourmet food store. We elbowed our way past black-clothed sham artists and zombied Eurotrash and made our way to the vegetable bins where we selected a Noah's manifest of the six varieties available that day: Idaho, yellow Finn, red organic, red Creamer, new, and Yukon gold. After figuring out a way to identify them after cooking (not as easy as you might think, especially if you're hungry) we boiled one set of samples and sautéed the other in sweet butter. The envelope, please:

RED ORGANIC
boiled: bland, namby-pamby, "standard potato" flavor
fried: not good, muddy and stagnant taste

RED CREAMER
boiled: firm, breaks rather than mashes in the mouth; good home fry material
fried: very firm, earthy (surprise, surprise)

NEW
boiled: rich gold color, earthy yet sweet; had soggiest edges
fried: very mushy, blandly sweet

YUKON GOLD
boiled: richest color, fastest cooker, very sticky in mouth; good for gnocchi
fried: extremely soft, not a good frying candidate

YELLOW FINN
boiled: smooth, fastest dispersal in mouth; salt brings out slight tartness
fried: crispy, firm, and mealy; frying promotes sweetness

IDAHO
boiled: THE CHAMP, firm and mealy; a classic potato with highest butter absorption (what else matters?)
fried: classic home fry

Three of us once had a dinner conversation centered on which starch of the mighty three—potatoes, pasta, and rice—we might pick if we'd be limited to only one for the rest of our lives. After some soul-searching and emotional duress, potatoes won by a slight margin. (We actually decided to each pick one, and share portions.)

As a footnote, after doing the taste test we drove 300 miles, slept, and found we were still full the next morning. Before breakfast.

●

MEAT LOAF
WITH MASHED POTATOES

Nowadays we see meat loaves made with all sorts of weird extenders; the hallowed bread crumb or chunk of white bread soaked in milk is being shunned. First it's whole wheat bread; from there it's just a hop to rolled oats, cracker crumbs, pearl barley, bulgur, and the catch-all of healthdom, oat bran.

Some people are going so far as to do away with extenders completely. If that's what you want, why not just have a hamburger? No, we've gotten accustomed to particles of some kind keeping those little meat molecules a proper distance from one another, and what could be better than our favorite food group, the potato? As far as we're concerned, that spring-time glint in a bull's eye is probably a bovine hologram of a large Idaho, swimming in butter.

The other meat loaf controversy is whether it should be baked in a loaf pan or shaped free-form as a long lump. It should be no surprise that we have an opinion on this too; we prefer loafing to taking our lumps. Plus, if you use a loaf pan you get perfect slices for sandwiches the next day.

    2 eggs
    ¾ cup milk
 1¼ pounds ground beef
    ¾ pound ground pork
    2 cups mashed potatoes, well buttered
    1 large red onion, chopped
    2 cloves garlic, minced
    ½ cup hot salsa
       salt and pepper

- Beat the eggs well with the milk. Mix everything in large bowl, using the hands to make sure all ingredients are well distributed. Pack into loaf pan and bake in 350° oven about 1½ hours.

● ●

CONSOMMÉ WITH SUET BALLS

(From *Mrs. Rorer's New Cook Book,* ca. 1900)

We suppose the question here is: Why? The answer is because it's there. We're also on the board of the Suet Preservation League. When we were little kids we used to watch our grandmother (no, the other one) stick chunks of suet up in trees for the winter birds. There used to be piles of it behind butchers' counters, and it was practically given away. Mincemeat was made from suet; pie crusts and cookies had it as a base.

Suet *is rapidly joining the ranks of words like* sweet, *loving, and* affection; *they're no longer politically correct, and we miss them as their sounds die out. Suet as substance is also becoming a nonentity. Cattle are increasingly being bred to have the body fat content of obsessive neurotics who do things like compete in triathlons. (For us, a triathlon is breakfast, lunch, and dinner.) What little is left is stripped from the carcass, rendered into blocks, and buried deep beneath the desert floor in Nevada, next to the spent nuclear fuel rods.*

Suet balls
 2 ounces of suet
 8 tablespoonfuls of flour
 I saltspoonful of salt
    A dash of pepper
 2 quarts of stock

* Nineteenth-century cookbook author Sarah Tyson Rorer gives these instructions: "Remove the membrane from the suet, chop fine, add the flour, and the salt and pepper; mix, and add sufficient ice water to just moisten, not to make it wet. Make into tiny balls, drop them into a little boiling stock, and cook slowly for five minutes. Put them into the soup tureen and pour over the hot stock."

● ●

BONED STUFFED CHICKEN IN BREAD DOUGH WITH VELOUTÉ SAUCE

This showstopper is related to an old Tuscan dish, pollo in pane, *in which the chicken is not boned, and is stuffed loosely with a few freshly sautéed vegetables. Being entertainers, we boned the bird, and added the gravity of fried potatoes and spinach.*

Actually, boning a chicken is a lot easier than it sounds. If you have a small very sharp knife and a pair of surgical scissors, that's half the battle. The rest is no more than the old carnival side-show trick of pressing nails into the sides of your eyeballs. If you know where your tear ducts are, the only other requirement is confidence. Just imagine that Mr. Gray wrote a companion volume on chicken anatomy, and follow the map. Slowly.

Chicken in a loaf of bread is a lot funnier if you can get it into the oven before any of the guests see it lolling around naked. Then, as you bring it to table, you can give a big sob story about how you're broke, how the roof needs patching, and the royalties are late again. Pick up a big knife, slice off the top third of the bread and reveal the bird. If no one laughs, you should probably think about your life.

 1 roasting chicken, about 7 pounds
 3 loaves frozen Italian bread dough
 5 medium boiling potatoes
11 tablespoons butter
12 ounces fresh spinach
 2 egg whites
   dash of nutmeg
 3 tablespoons heavy cream
   salt and pepper

- Wash and dry chicken. Cut off wings at elbow joints, then bone the entire chicken, leaving skin unbroken.

- Defrost the bread dough. Peel potatoes and cut in ⅜-inch dice. Parboil until half done in salted water, then sauté until light brown in 3 tablespoons of the butter.
- Clean and steam the spinach. Press out excess liquid, then chop finely. Beat the egg whites until frothy, then mix well with the spinach, along with a dash of nutmeg, the heavy cream, and salt and pepper to taste.
- Place chicken on its back and stuff with the potatoes, then with a layer of spinach. Sew body incision shut. Melt the remaining 8 tablespoons butter until bubbling, then brown chicken, cooking about 8 minutes each on back and breast side. Be very careful when turning bird. Let cool about 20 minutes.
- Knead the loaves of dough into one ball. Roll or stretch out to thickness of a pizza. Place chicken breast-side down on dough; gather dough around bird and press edges together in seam along back. Place seam-side down in oiled roasting pan.
- Bake at 400° for 10 minutes, then 1½ hours at 325°. Serve with Velouté Sauce, below.

VELOUTÉ SAUCE

     3 tablespoons butter
     3 tablespoons flour
  1½ cups chicken stock
     1 cup light cream
   ⅛ teaspoon dry mustard
   ⅛ teaspoon turmeric
        salt and pepper

- Melt butter in saucepan until foam subsides. Add flour and cook until mixture loses its raw smell. Bring stock to boil and add to roux, stirring with whisk or spoon until bubbling and smooth. Let cook a few minutes until thickened, then add light cream and spices. Cook to desired consistency.

●　●

POTATO-CRUSTED FRIED CHICKEN

Last year we spent some time on an editor's nickel browsing in a junk shop in Berlin, on Maryland's Eastern Shore, home to about 2.4 billion pounds of America's chickens. We picked up a ladies' church group cookbook and noticed a variation on this gem. The original used the very fine type of instant potato; we think using the so-called buds adds to the texture. And gravy made from fat and potato is certainly a first for us.

About five miles north, we stopped at a small cemetery by the side of the road. At least 15 percent of the headstones said "Perdue." Sooner or later even the tough get gone.

    1   3- to 4-pound chicken, cut up for frying
    ½   cup lard
    2   eggs
    2   cups instant potato buds
    1   cup chicken stock
        salt and pepper

- Wash and dry chicken pieces. Heat lard in large frying pan until melted and hot. Beat eggs together; coat chicken first with egg, then potato buds. Fry in lard until light brown, turning frequently. Do not crowd pan. Pour out about ⅔ of the lard.
- Sprinkle any leftover potato buds over chicken and remaining fat. Add stock, cover tightly, and simmer about 15 minutes. Season with salt and pepper.

MOZZARELLA PIE

This originated in a one-line newspaper description of a similar dish. It was nearing dinner, so all we had to do was stop in at Grace's cheese store and then lift the lid on our custom-made 500-pound potato bin.

Owing to the intense creaminess of this dish, it really should stand for a bit before serving so it can be scooped out with something flatter than a large soupspoon.

    3 pounds potatoes, about 10 medium
    5 ounces salami, finely diced
   12 ounces mozzarella (preferably fresh), shredded
    6 tablespoons butter, plus additional for buttering pan
    8 ounces ricotta
    3 eggs
   ¾ teaspoon pepper
    1 medium red onion, finely diced
   ½ cup fresh bread crumbs
   ¼ cup Parmesan

- Peel and quarter potatoes and boil in water to cover until tender. Drain well and return briefly to low heat to evaporate excess water. Mash well, but do not whip.
- Add salami and mozzarella and stir until cheese forms thin threads. Add 4 tablespoons of the butter and stir until melted. Stir in ricotta, then add eggs, one at a time, stirring until well blended. Add black pepper and onion and mix well.
- Butter large baking dish and coat sides and bottom with bread crumbs, shaking out excess crumbs. Add potato mixture to dish, sprinkle with Parmesan, and dot with remaining 2 tablespoons butter. Bake in preheated 350° oven 30 minutes, or until nicely browned. Let stand 10 minutes before serving.

● ●

POTATOES WITH EXTRA-VIRGIN OLIVE OIL, GARLIC, AND ROSEMARY

A few years back, we went up to Quebec City for the annual winter Carnival. It's a jolly, loony affair, highlighted by snow sculpture competitions, a canoe race across the half-frozen St. Lawrence, and the remarkable ability of thousands of Quebeckers to stand enthralled in minus 20° weather while a local politician takes half an hour to announce the Carnival Queen. The official tipple of this cryogenic shindig is something called caribou, a mixture of grain alcohol and cheap red wine (years ago, we're told, it had caribou blood in it) that seems to have something to do with the Carnival Queen Announcement Endurance Contest. We know, we know, alcohol only creates the illusion of warmth, and you're not supposed to drink when you're cold. That's what we keep hearing, from people who don't even drink when they're warm.

Still, man doesn't get through the Quebec night on caribou alone, which is why our favorite restaurant up there serves these spuds. We modified the recipe to specify extra-virgin. as the sautéing medium, just so the potatoes have a bit more presence. We'll announce the queen in a minute; first let us tell you, citoyens, *how nice it is to be here . . .*

- 6 medium boiling potatoes
- 6 tablespoons extra-virgin olive oil
- 2 cloves garlic, crushed
- 1 teaspoon dried rosemary
- salt and pepper

- Peel potatoes and cut in ½-inch dice. Cover with salted water and bring to boil; boil 5 minutes, remove from heat and drain. Dry thoroughly on paper towels. Heat the oil in a large skillet and add potatoes and garlic. Sprinkle with rosemary, salt, and plenty of pepper. Sauté until crispy.

CHAPTER 3

THE GOSPEL OF OF HEAVY CREAM

WHEN WAS THE last time you had a good belt of heavy cream? Not half-and-half, or light or medium or whipping cream, but the real thing. We're not talking about sneaking a sip from the bottom of the carton after you've made whipped cream, but actually pouring some into a glass and drinking it down like you would a cold beer on a hot day. If you recoil in horror at the thought, it's doubtful that your reaction is based on what you anticipate the taste would be like. No, it's because you've been snookered into believing that just two gulps into that glass, you'd be down on the floor as dead as if you'd just had a Drano malted. At the very least, you're certain, your new Hugo Boss suit would have to go to the Salvation Army.

Well, maybe—if you followed this regimen every day. Or maybe not. But the fact is, you know that cream would taste good. Of course it would. Heavy cream is the linchpin of classic French cooking, the glory of American farmhouse cuisine, and the original food for which the term "mouth feel" was invented. We owe it to ourselves to let up just a bit on our new national habit of cream-dread, and to remember why there are phrases like "cream of the crop," and "skimming off the cream." Instead of tolerating cream only when it appears as part of desserts labeled "sinful," get reacquainted with cream sauces, with what cream does for potatoes, and with its ability to transform even such a dull dish as spinach.

But start by drinking a glass—maybe at a party, in front of your friends. It'll be fun listening to them try to talk you into handing over your car keys.

• •

KILLER NOG

Now that the federal government has told a leading brewing company that it can't base the name and ad campaign of a malt liquor on the product's alcoholic kick, we feel somewhat hesitant to tag a label like "Killer Nog" onto a cheery and beloved yuletide concoction. But we'll do it anyway, out of respect for tradition. During one holiday season in the early eighties, one of us unveiled this elixir at his annual eggnog-and-cookies bash in Newburyport, Massachusetts. Among the guests was one of the town's heartiest celebrators, a man remembered to this day for once delivering the deadpan line, "I don't drink as much as I do." He took a hefty glug of the stuff, lowered his punch cup, and said, beaming, "That's Killer Nog!" And Killer Nog it has been ever since.

We have two options for serving this recipe at your holiday revels. One is to ration out one cup per guest. The other is to make enough to float a Cunard liner, and dig out your supply of extra blankets and sleeping bags when you're rummaging in the cellar for the punch bowl. Hint: Option two is a lot more fun.

10　eggs, separated
⅓　cup sugar, powdered or superfine
1　quart heavy cream
1　750-milliliter bottle of cognac (V.S. will do nicely)
1½　cups rum, dark if you prefer a heartier eggnog
2　cups milk
　　freshly ground nutmeg

- Beat egg whites and sugar until they are foamy, almost at the soft-peak stage. Beat yolks in a separate bowl until they drip from the beater in a thick, bright yellow ribbon (this recipe is suitable for military homecomings). Now pour the egg white mixture into the yolks and beat with an electric mixer until nicely combined, about 3 minutes.
- Using the bowl you will serve the eggnog in, beat the cream until it barely holds soft peaks. With the mixer running at medium speed, slowly add the beaten egg mixture, then the cognac, rum, and milk. Garnish with nutmeg, and chill for 4 hours. If eggnog appears thicker at the top than the bottom, stir gently just before serving.

ATHOLL BROSE

Every now and then, a genteel controversy breezes up in the readers' column in Gourmet. *For some reason, these little set-tos often involve recipes from cuisines that are virtually off the culinary map—after all, Italians have no need to squabble about the correct way to make lasagna, since Italians all know that there are about 11,000 ways to make lasagna and they are all correct. But you take a subject like Scottish cooking, and it's a different story.*

This particular debate wasn't about cooking, but about drinking—to wit, it was about a potation called Atholl Brose. A woman wrote in August of 1975, seeking a particular restaurant's recipe for a dessert by that name, which Gourmet *found and printed. It was a mixture of whipped cream, honey, and scotch, to be eaten with a spoon. Six issues later, a Scot took issue with this version, claiming that Atholl Brose—a favorite of Highland foot regiments, he claimed—should be concocted only from scotch, honey, and water in which oatmeal had steeped.*

We didn't take sides in this altercation, because we were already partisans of yet another interpretation of Atholl Brose—one that, oddly enough, had appeared in Gourmet *three years earlier. It has cream and oatmeal, and we have modified it so that it can be served as a thick, eggnog-like drink instead of as a dessert. We'd like to think that this will make all Scots happy, but they are a contentious lot.*

- 1 cup oatmeal (rolled, not steel cut)
- ¾ cup water
- 3 cups scotch
- ½ cup honey
- 6 cups heavy cream

- Soak the oatmeal in the water for 30 minutes. Using a food processor fitted with the steel blade, pulse the oatmeal mixture until the cereal is chopped fine. Mix thoroughly with scotch and honey and set aside. In a separate bowl, beat the cream until it doubles in volume but is still pourable. Slowly add the scotch mixture, beating constantly until Atholl Brose has the consistency of thick eggnog. For serving instructions, see Killer Nog, above.

• •

FETTUCINI ALFREDO

For many of us, this was the first Italian dish we ever encountered that wasn't made with tomatoes and garlic—sort of like meeting your first blonde, blue-eyed Italian. It's always a hit as an accompaniment to grilled meats, with a nice salad on the side; but if you're on a diet, you can eat it all by itself.

 1 pound fettucini, regular or spinach (fresh is best)
 4 tablespoons butter
 ¾ cup freshly grated Parmesan or Romano cheese, or a
       mixture of the two
     freshly grated black pepper
 1 cup heavy cream

• As salted water for fettucini is approaching the boil, melt butter in small saucepan, and pour into a large mixing bowl. Add cheese to butter; stir. Cook fettucini al dente and drain immediately; do not allow to cool. Turn fettucini into butter and cheese mixture and toss vigorously with large salad forks. Add grated black pepper to taste (we like lots) as you toss. Continue tossing while adding heavy cream until the consistency you desire is reached. Ideally, Fettucini Alfredo should be moist, with all cheese melted into the butter and cream, and no dryness to the noodles; but when you are finished serving, there should be no puddle of cream at the bottom of the bowl.

• •

PORK IN MUSTARD-CREAM SAUCE

We dreamed this up during a charming stretch in northwest Vermont when the thermometer never found the energy to rise much above zero for a week. Luckily, the car started so we could keep our pork supply up.

Every morning the sky would be dark gray. By noon it would be light gray, then back to dark gray at three, then black at five. The yellows of the mustard and the flames were an attempt to add some color to our existence. As Pierre Bonnard said, "You can't have too much yellow."

The combination of mustard, white wine, garlic, distilled spirits, and heavy cream is a fairly standard routine for northwest France. It works well with just about any cut of fresh pork, as well as chicken. To cook a tenderloin in one piece, for instance, the only real change would be to lengthen the cooking time. We've always been in favor of the inexact sciences.

- 3 tablespoons peanut oil
- 1 tablespoon butter
- 1 clove garlic, crushed
- 6 ¾-inch tenderloin medallions of pork
- ⅓ cup dry white wine
- ⅓ cup cider
- 3 tablespoons cognac or calvados
- 1 tablespoon Dijon mustard
- ⅔ cup heavy cream
  salt and pepper
- ¼ cup minced parsley

- Heat oil and butter in large skillet; add garlic and sauté lightly, about 3 or 4 minutes. Meanwhile, place medallions on cutting board and pound lightly with heel of hand. The object is to break down the meat fibers a bit, not make it thin enough to read the classifieds through. When garlic has cooked a bit, add medallions to pan and brown on medium heat, about 3 minutes per side. Add wine and cider, bring to boil, reduce to simmer, cover and cook 10 minutes.
- Heat a serving platter. Remove medallions to platter and cover loosely with foil. Remove and discard garlic, turn heat to high and reduce liquids to ⅓ volume, stirring and scraping up particles from pan. Put meat back in skillet and turn pieces to cover with liquid. Add cognac or calvados, heat briefly and ignite with match. Turn your face while doing this or you'll resemble a Norman farmer who's spent too much time doing quality control on the calvados. Cook until flames die out. Add Dijon mustard, the heavy cream, and salt and pepper. Cook about 5 minutes until the cream thickens.
- Transfer meat to platter, pour sauce over all, and garnish with parsley.

CREAM BISCUITS

Joe's Dairy, on Sullivan Street at the edge of New York's Little Italy, pops up in our conversations all the time, as in "Well, I'll be going past Grace's so I'll pick up a fresh mozzarella" or "Don't forget to stop at Grace's for the ricotta and some Sardo." (Grace is the majorette-domo of the place; her specialty is handing out small chunks of smoked mozzarella in the manner of Dr. Pavlov.)

Besides being the home of just about any kind of cheese we'd ever want to eat, Joe's is also the spot where we first saw heavy cream in quart containers. They reminded us of fonts of holy water for a new religion.

These biscuits can substitute for communion wafers. Having given us a reason to buy the heavy quarts, they're great spread with butter, or covered with a whitish, pasty sauce studded with nuggets of sausage meat, (see Biscuits and Gravy, page 18) or, on a good day, spread with butter and then covered with the sausage sauce.

> 4 cups flour
>   large dash of salt
> 2 teaspoons baking powder
> ¾ cup butter, chilled
> I quart heavy cream

- Sift flour with salt and baking powder. Cut butter in small pieces and work into the flour with a pastry cutter. Add cream and knead a few minutes. Roll to ¼-inch thickness, cut in 2-inch rounds. Bake at 400° about 15 minutes or until lightly browned.

● ●

SAM 'N' ELLA'S EGG SALAD IN A JAR

Our friends Sam and Ella used to run a small restaurant in Chicopee, Massachusetts. Their taste ran parallel to ours, with a healthy emphasis on the five main food groups: potatoes, rice, pasta, garlic, and olive oil. Unfortunately, while their master recipe for egg salad defined haute cuisine in Chicopee, it also defined several violations of the local health code.

Fear of salmonella bacteria seems to have replaced the fear of being uncool in the "aware" set; it's now okay to tell raunchy ethnic jokes but God forbid you should be seen dropping a couple of raw eggs onto a nice plate of steak tartare. As our grandmother used to say, perhaps watching a dead oak miss the rosebushes only to turn the chicken coop into a one-room flat, "If it's not this, it's that."

This dish, however, is pretty safe. Hard-boiled eggs are cooked past the survival temperature of salmonella; commercial mayonnaise has an acidity level set by USDA edict specifically to eliminate the bacteria. Plus, you don't have to dirty the Tupperware.

8 hard-boiled eggs, chopped
1 small red onion, minced
   salt and pepper
1 32-ounce jar mayonnaise, with about ¼ mayonnaise
      remaining

- Add eggs, onion, and salt and pepper to jar. Using strong wooden spoon, stir like hell. Best technique is to stir from bottom, making sure you get the mayonnaise in the bottom groove. Use immediately, or simply replace lid on jar and refrigerate until needed.

● ●

SPINACH GNOCCHI WITH THREE-CHEESE SAUCE

This is a variation on a dish we first encountered during a press junket to Geneva—one of those miserable jobs that somebody has to do. Actually, most people don't realize just how much work it is to be escorted around glamorous foreign cities while not spending any money. Earlier in the Day Of The Gnocchi, we had been taken to a trade center and shown a filmstrip on the machine-tool industry, and then escorted through a string of historic buildings by a tour guide who had been vaccinated with a phonograph needle. Finally, we got to see the famous monument to the heroes of the Reformation. After staring at a statue of John Calvin—and having it stare back—you need a dish like gnocchi with three-cheese sauce to put you back in the proper voluptuary's perspective on life.

    2 pounds potatoes, peeled and quartered
    12 ounces fresh spinach
    2 egg yolks
    3 tablespoons Parmesan
       salt
    ⅓ cup flour

• Boil the potatoes until soft, drain, then mash or rice through a colander. Wash spinach and put in saucepan without drying. Cover and bring to boil; cook a few minutes until completely wilted. Drain very well, pressing as much water out as possible. Chop finely. Add to bowl with other ingredients and mix well, then knead briefly on floured board. With hands, roll into a long rope the thickness of a finger. Cut into 1½-inch pieces. (If you want to be fancy, you can run the dough through a gnocchi machine.) Bring a large amount of cold water to a boil and add gnocchi, about 12 at a time.

Skim from pot when they rise to surface. Repeat until all are cooked. Toss with warm Three-Cheese Sauce, below.

•

THREE-CHEESE SAUCE

½ cup butter
⅔ cup grated Parmesan
1½ cups heavy cream
¼ pound Gorgonzola
3 ounces Mascarpone

- Melt butter in large skillet, then stir in Parmesan and cook over low heat until cheese is melted. Add 1 cup of the cream and simmer, stirring, until well blended. Add Gorgonzola and Mascarpone and stir until melted. Blend in additional cream to reach desired consistency, and bring to simmer. Makes enough to sauce about 1½ pounds pasta, preferably spinach gnocchi.

● ●

TURKEY GRAVY

We had a bad run of luck with turkey gravy back in the early eighties. Three Thanksgivings in a row, events conspired to deny us its core ingredient, good turkey broth. The first year, somebody who was "helping in the kitchen" threw out the neck and giblets. The second year, the broth got made, but somebody figured it wasn't anything important, poured it down the drain, and washed the pot. And the year after that, the broth got made, strained, and transferred to a handmade pottery bowl that somebody liked too much to throw away, even though it had broken in nine places and been repaired with cheap model airplane glue. We were carrying it from counter to table when the glue gave way, inundating our new flannel pants and scalding the shine off a nice pair of Cole-Haans.

All of these somebodies have been permanently barred, we are pleased to say, from any involvement in the preparation of turkey gravy. It's a simple recipe, but we suggest that you screen your staff carefully.

    neck and giblets
1 medium onion, peeled and coarsely chopped
2 stalks celery, coarsely chopped
2 carrots, peeled and coarsely chopped
    salt and pepper
1 cup light cream
    fat and juices from roasted turkey, in roasting pan
4 tablespoons flour
2 tablespoons cognac

- Make stock by putting neck and giblets in saucepan with vegetables, salt and pepper, and 1 quart cold water. Bring to boil and simmer for 2 hours. Drain, reserving stock, neck and giblets. Finely chop the giblets, shred meat from neck, and set aside.

- Bring strained stock and cream to a boil in separate pans. Pour off fat from your turkey's roasting pan, leaving 4 or 5 tablespoons fat. Add any cooking juices to stock. Place roaster on stovetop (it usually takes two burners). Heat fat and add flour, stirring constantly. Cook several minutes at medium heat. Add 1 cup stock to flour, then the cream. Continue cooking to thicken. Add additional stock to adjust consistency. When desired thickness is reached, add cognac, neck meat, and giblets. Add salt and pepper to taste. Cook for 2 minutes and serve.

● ●

CHICKEN, CALVADOS, AND CREAM

Some may accuse us of padding the manuscript, but this switchover makes the point that there's not that much new under the culinary sun. The old reliables are just that. After all, when you consider that a chicken looks just like a smaller, two legged, winged and feathered pig, there's all the reason in the world to cook them the same way.

　　ingredients for Pork in Mustard-Cream Sauce, page 52,
　　　　minus pork medallions
　3　chicken breasts, split

- See directions for Pork in Mustard-Cream Sauce. When we say pork, think chicken. Proceed as directed.

● ●

CREAMED SPINACH

Here we have spinach's leap at immortality. We like spinach—at least one of us does—but even that one will agree that most people find it a tedious, Protestant sort of vegetable. Well, here's how to bring it around. If we could figure out a way to make broccoli or cauliflower absorb this much heavy cream, we would.

3 pounds fresh spinach, washed, with coarse stems removed
1 cup heavy cream
   dash of freshly grated nutmeg
1 hard-boiled egg yolk

- Steam spinach until just tender, about 2 or 3 minutes in or over boiling salted water. Strain spinach, pressing firmly against sides of colander to remove as much water as possible. Put cooked spinach on board and chop as finely as possible. Turn spinach into a sauté pan over low heat, and begin adding cream gradually, pouring in a little more each time the previous pouring has been absorbed by the spinach. Add dash of nutmeg as you pour in the cream. The spinach will slowly lighten in color and become fluffy as the cream is absorbed. When all of the cream is absorbed, turn the spinach onto a heated platter and arrange in a circular pattern, gently flattening the top. Press the hard-boiled egg yolk through a sieve, and garnish the spinach with the sieved egg.

● ●

FROM WHENCE
THEY CAME

●

WE'VE ALWAYS THOUGHT that the Bible was a pretty good companion to any kind of serious thought; it's also a great reference work. Consider, for example, Genesis 5: "This is the book of the generations of Adam. When God created man, he made him in the likeness of God." Well, when man got around to creating food, he had to start somewhere too. Over the centuries lots of cuisines have come and, usually blessedly, gone. In our hearts we may be culinary fundamentalists, but who wants to dine on leg of sloth or pickled mastodon ears?

Personally, our brief adult life spans seem to have covered a particularly intense succession of silliness, probably aided by America's increasing dependence on mass media as a source of meaningful wisdom. That same media, however, missed reporting on one of the most important meals of the last several decades. In the spring of 1968, a number of shadowy figures crept into Chicago's Old Town. The Democratic Convention was approaching and plans were being hatched that would prove to be in conflict with Mayor Daley's dreams. Being a revolutionary takes up a lot of energy, and one night two of the leaders met at a small veggie/health-food restaurant on Wells Street to coin some new slogans and try to imagine what the working class actually was. Slogans come and slogans go; what remains with us is the fallout from Abbie and Jerry's dinner.

The fare was simple enough to make oatmeal with brown sugar and raisins look like a big production. Glasses of water at their sides, the leaders of the new emerging order had bowls of

GENEALOGY OF ST

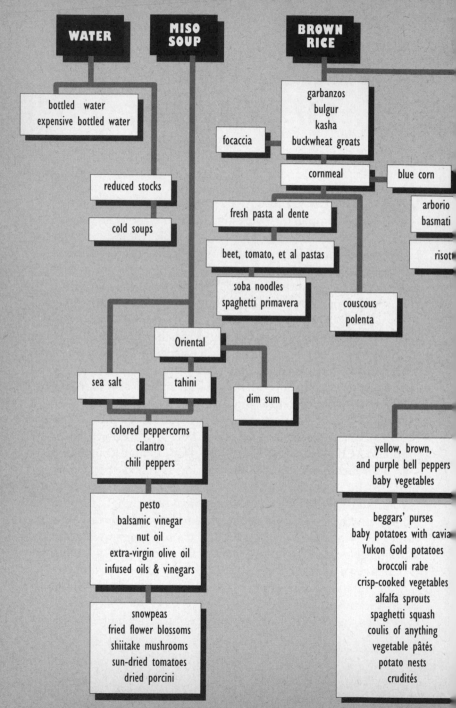

WATER

MISO SOUP

BROWN RICE

bottled water
expensive bottled water

garbanzos
bulgur
kasha
buckwheat groats

focaccia

cornmeal

blue corn

reduced stocks

arborio
basmati

fresh pasta al dente

cold soups

beet, tomato, et al pastas

risot

soba noodles
spaghetti primavera

Oriental

couscous
polenta

sea salt

tahini

dim sum

colored peppercorns
cilantro
chili peppers

yellow, brown,
and purple bell peppers
baby vegetables

pesto
balsamic vinegar
nut oil
extra-virgin olive oil
infused oils & vinegars

beggars' purses
baby potatoes with cavia
Yukon Gold potatoes
broccoli rabe
crisp-cooked vegetables
alfalfa sprouts
spaghetti squash
coulis of anything
vegetable pâtés
potato nests
crudités

snowpeas
fried flower blossoms
shiitake mushrooms
sun-dried tomatoes
dried porcini

PID FOOD TRICKS

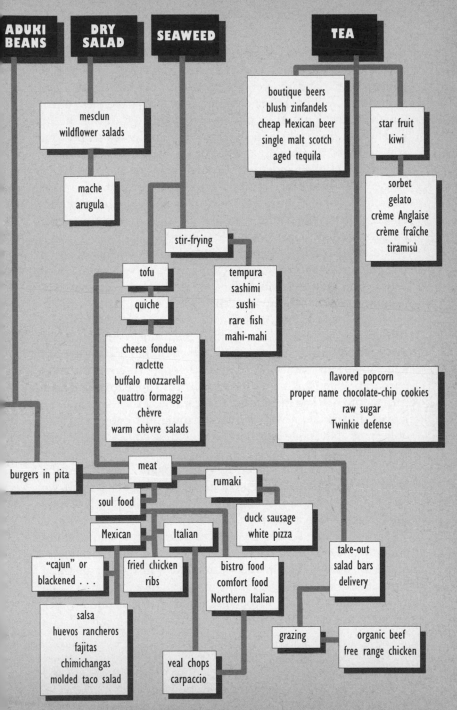

ADUKI BEANS

DRY SALAD

SEAWEED

TEA

boutique beers
blush zinfandels
cheap Mexican beer
single malt scotch
aged tequila

star fruit
kiwi

mesclun
wildflower salads

sorbet
gelato
crème Anglaise
crème fraîche
tiramisù

mache
arugula

stir-frying

tofu

tempura
sashimi
sushi
rare fish
mahi-mahi

quiche

cheese fondue
raclette
buffalo mozzarella
quattro formaggi
chèvre
warm chèvre salads

flavored popcorn
proper name chocolate-chip cookies
raw sugar
Twinkie defense

burgers in pita

meat

rumaki

soul food

duck sausage
white pizza

Mexican

Italian

take-out
salad bars
delivery

"cajun" or
blackened . . .

fried chicken
ribs

bistro food
comfort food
Northern Italian

salsa
huevos rancheros
fajitas
chimichangas
molded taco salad

grazing

organic beef
free range chicken

veal chops
carpaccio

miso soup, a dry salad of tattered organic greens, then the main course: chipped plates covered with masses of brown rice, adzuki beans, and seaweed. (They were big on the masses.) Everything was boiled or steamed and fairly colorless, but it was pure. They ate, they planned, they left. From this fateful meal came the truth, and the truth is represented as best we can in the accompanying chart. This is where it started.

We should make a few observations on the subliminal causes and effects of politics on food. Most of the food the so-called counterculture ate had two characteristics: It was different from what their parents ate (the same parents that paid for the tuition at Columbia and the VW minibuses), and it was evocative of the Third World, which stood for purity of thought and intent. To anyone who's actually been to the Third World, this is at best laughable; at worst it's patronizing and preposterous. But those were the sixties, bless 'em.

Time passed; Nixon became president and long-hairs started getting jobs. Naturally they held on to their pure-as-driven-snow ideals, and America's restaurants and supermarkets changed with the times. People discovered food preparation and the wok sprang forth. Tofu appeared, and later turned into fish and meat. Like the miracle of the fishes and the loaves, things had a way of transforming just enough so that adherents of the politically correct mealtime could pretend they were still religious.

Then the religion turned towards wealth, greed, and the good life. Hippies changed a couple of letters and suddenly we had yuppies. Straying a bit from Third World worship, anything eaten in France or Italy became okay, just as the beloved VW grew into the adored BMW. The Third World came off the pedestal and was replaced by the third car (or the third home, or the third trip to Vail in one season). Now just about anything was okay to eat as long as it met two conditions: it had to be expensive, and it had to be unknown to the economic tier below yours. Beef had to be organic, and chickens had to be free-range. Since fish were already organic and free-range, the folks in charge decided to cook them only to the point of being barely edible. You were supposed to be hip enough to know that was the way they *should* be cooked.

Will the circle be unbroken? Of course, since none of this stuff was what we'd call particularly original in the first place. All that's happened is that the train, steaming along the circular tracks, has inexorably come up on its own caboose. Ralph Lauren ads show bored long-faced models wearing what look to be "work" jackets, along with clothing that has the American flag displayed proudly on the chest instead of snidely on the seat of a pair of bell-bottoms. Minute Rice is making a comeback, and restaurants that used to pride themselves on the thinness of their carpaccio slices now crow about the lumps in their mashed potatoes. So check out the family tree, and if the good old days press hard upon you, shed a tear for good old brown rice. It will save us the trouble.

●

CHAPTER 4

IF IT CAN BE POACHED, IT CAN BE FRIED

SOME MANUFACTURER OF a low-fat cooking medium recently ran an ad campaign that lamented the fact that even though people were buying lean cuts of meat, rediscovering fish, and taking the skin off of chicken, they were still frying these delectables in butter and oil. Of course they were! These things taste good, and they enhance the flavor of whatever you fry in them. We don't know about the low-fat sprays—we always get them mixed up with bug repellent—but we have performed experiments designed to compare frying with the ultimate low-fat (or rather no-fat) cooking method: poaching. Our control item was the potato. We sliced and french fried potatoes, then took an identical group of spuds and poached them. Our conclusion was that the french fries tasted a lot better, and that the only way to redeem the poached potatoes was to mash them and drench them in butter. (This is not to be confused with our potato taste test, page 37, in which butter figured right from the start in both presentations.)

Nevertheless, we'd like to make our contribution to the lite spirit of the age by suggesting frying media other than that old devil butter. To wit, poultry fat and lard.

Poor lard has gotten a bad rap. You wouldn't think to look at it, all snow-white and innocent, but people actually think that it's bad for them. This probably has something to do with the misappropriation of the word for use as a synonym for excess human poundage, but then a lot of perfectly good words have been misappropriated of late. It's time to rediscover lard.

When you get it to the right temperature, it causes no undue grease absorption in the food being fried, leaves no aftertaste, and won't stain your pants any worse than canola oil. Best of all, as Diana Kennedy points out in *The Art of Mexican Cooking*, it's actually a low-cholesterol way to fry stuff. Yes. According to Kennedy, lard contains 10 percent cholesterol, while butter has 22 percent. She goes on to say that you needn't use as much lard as butter, since it doesn't burn at high temperature. "The flavor of homemade lard is incomparable," Kennedy rhapsodizes, and that's as brave and honest a statement as we've seen in any cookbook these past few years.

Chickens and geese are also valuable sources of cooking fat. Chicken fat, aka schmaltz, is a handy frying medium for those denied lard for religious reasons; what's more, you can spread it on rye bread, something few people do outside Eastern Europe. As for geese, they are regular fat mines. Never buy a goose without rendering the fat, which actually rates one cholesterol point lower than lard. For instructions, follow the steps for chicken fat on page 115. You'll never waste goose fat again.

●   ●

WASP PIROGI

Around 1986 we contracted to test some recipes for a cookbook writer who had never bothered to develop a sense of humor. Well, we got to laugh a lot. We also got to spend someone else's money on things like Real Sauternes (!) and Two Pounds of Fresh Foie Gras! There's nothing to cheer us up like sorting through two hundred pounds of fresh goose liver looking for the perfect couple to catch our fancy.

We had a big dinner party, cooked all the food, and asked our guests for any comments. When we served this dish, the

*only comment, besides "amazing," was "pirogi for WASPs."
Ever mindful of our pocketbooks, if not of others', we made a
few changes: the chunks of goose liver have turned into
chicken livers, the soaking in sauternes has been eliminated,
and the strips of home-cured Smithfield ham have changed
into prosciutto.*

*The pirogi were a big hit at our annual Eve of New Year's
Eve party, where they disappeared like anything not nailed
down in New York City.*

> 1 pound fresh goose liver (chicken livers if you're poor)
> 1 bottle *real* sauternes (omit if you're using chicken livers)
> ¾ pound Smithfield ham, thinly sliced (prosciutto if you're
>   poor)
> 2 packages frozen puff pastry
>   vegetable oil for deep frying

• Trim fat and membranes from liver. Slice into 1-inch cubes
and marinate overnight in sauternes. Wrap each liver in a
thin slice of ham. Thaw puff pastry and cut sheets into
oblongs about 2 inches by 4 inches. Place a wrapped liver on
one side of dough, brush edges with cold water, then fold
over and press firmly to seal. Heat at least 3 inches of oil in
a deep fryer or heavy pot to 375° and fry pirogi, a few at a
time, until golden. Drain on paper towels and serve hot.

● ●

CRAB CAKES
WITH CAUL FAT

A lot of useful phobias, such as fear of opening letters from the IRS and fear of standing on steep rocky cliffs during an ice storm, can and have been overcome. Everybody's got to be afraid of something, though, and the monster stalking in the modern moors is fear of frying. "Duck, Honey, there's a Frialator in there!" Diners lose their color when they spot empty five-gallon tins of frying medium on the sidewalk in front of what they used to think was a good restaurant. Cooks lose their life savings trying to open fish and chip shops in places like Harvard Square or towns like Burlington, Vermont.

After years of going our own way we've decided to join the trend. For one recipe, yes, Chris and Bill get off their low horse to mix with the flock.

We've taken a Mid-Atlantic icon, the Maryland crab cake, and made it politically correct. No frying. That's right: we have the first recipe for crab cakes that doesn't include coating the thing with bread crumbs and frying it in disgusting, oily fat.

The problem is holding the cake together while it cooks. The answer, like that to so many culinary questions, lies in France. Simply refer to your crab cake as a crêpinette. Get a piece of caul fat (as in "born with a caul . . . "), the membrane of fat that lines a pig's visceral cavity: it looks like a poorly made lace shawl, woven from pork fat. Just cut a piece big enough to cover your cakes and you can broil them, knowing they'll hold their shape and also self-baste. Eat Healthy and Live Longer.

1 pound crabmeat
¼ cup mayonnaise
¼ cup minced parsley
½ teaspoon salt
¾ teaspoon pepper
1 tablespoon Worcestershire
½ teaspoon dry mustard
1 egg, beaten
   caul fat

- Flake crabmeat into mixing bowl, discarding any shell shards. Add all ingredients except fat and mix well. Stop before it turns to mush. Shape into 4 oval cakes.
- Cut pieces of caul fat large enough to completely envelop cakes. Place seam-side down on broiling pan and broil until well browned. Turn carefully and cook other side.

DEEP FAT FRYING

DEEP-FRIED
SWEET POTATO BALLS

Last Thanksgiving some friends served a casserole of this delectable sweet potato–Gorgonzola puree. Heady with the perfume of cheese bacteria mixed with garlic, we started thinking: How can we take this further? A need for New Year's Eve appetizers provided the answer.

Aware of the tendency of mashed potatoes to stiffen as they cool (see caveat, Perfect Mashed Potatoes, page 35), we made a batch of the sweet-potato-Gorgonzola mixture and tossed it into the refrigerator. A few hours later, they were stiff enough to roll into Titlelists. For the first batch we just rolled them in bread crumbs and dropped them into hot oil.

There is something to be said for pretesting: those first six balls slowly disappeared in the deep fryer. We kept digging them out with a strainer, but they never browned. They just got smaller and smaller. When they got to the size of BBs, we turned off the stove and sat down and thought.

Where had they gone? We've deep-fried a lot of food before but it always vanished after cooking. Finally we realized that, with all the cheese and butter in the mixture, what we were doing was trying to deep-fry butter.

No problem. A short sojourn in the freezer, a brief bath in beaten eggs, and a roll in the crumbs resulted in the birth of sweet potato Kiev. Watch the dribbles.

    4 pounds sweet potatoes
    ¾ cup butter
    ½ pound Gorgonzola
    6 cloves garlic, unpeeled
    2 teaspoons freshly ground black pepper
    3 eggs
    2 to 3 cups bread crumbs
       vegetable oil for deep-frying

- Put whole potatoes in pot with water to cover and boil until tender. Slip off skins and mash thoroughly in mixing bowl. Do not whip. While potatoes are still hot, add ½ cup of the butter and the Gorgonzola, cut in small pieces. Continue to mash until melted.

- Meanwhile, place unpeeled garlic cloves in small saucepan with remaining ¼ cup butter and ½ cup water. Bring to simmer and cook, covered, about 25 minutes, until garlic is very soft. Drain, slit skins, and squeeze out garlic paste. Add to potato mixture with the black pepper. Mix thoroughly. Refrigerate until mixture is stiff, at least 3 hours.

- With hands, form potato mixture into small balls, about ¾ inches in diameter. Place on baking sheet and freeze 2 hours.

- Beat eggs well in shallow bowl. Remove balls from freezer; coat with egg, then roll in bread crumbs to coat well and completely.

- Heat oil in deep fryer or heavy pot to 375°. Fry 6 or 8 balls at a time until well browned and drain on paper towels. If not served immediately, they may be kept at room temperature for several hours and reheated in a 400° oven for about 10 minutes.

• •

DEEP-FRIED CODFISH BALLS

Codfish balls are a great excuse to visit your local Italian or Greek grocery and pick up a long, smelly, dried cod fillet. If you've never seen one, look for an object that looks like a shard of plywood that was run over enough times on the interstate to become somewhat pliable. Looks can be deceiving; by the time it's been soaked and boiled, you're hungry.

A longtime staple of Jamaican restaurants, these balls can absorb wide variations of cayenne and black pepper. We sometimes wish that the "light" brigade, in its rush to give every dish the mean density of Styrofoam, would consider the role of pepper. A couple of teaspoons of black pepper counteracts what the more dainty among us perceive as excessively rich; maybe they spend so much time juggling the spicy morsel back and forth in their mouths they never realize they're devouring fish, potato, and butter.

This might be a good time to look at the thin versus thick batter debate. Some people totally eschew any batter thicker than a couple of hairs, and might as well shrink-wrap their friables. On the other side of the street, in Extender Land, they're eating a wad of greasy dough with . . . shrimp? Or is it a Vienna sausage? Who knows? Who cares?

In general, figure the smoother the substance coated, the lighter the batter. The preceding sweet potato balls would be absurd in a quarter inch of egg and baking powder batter. In the same vein, a healthy chunk of fresh haddock can stand up to a lot of insulation. If you're not sure, just remember form follows function: the outside should never be so thick that you can't guess the inside from across a normal living room.

Balls

  1 piece salt cod, about 1½ pounds
  6 medium potatoes
 ¼ cup milk
  4 tablespoons butter
  4 eggs
  1 teaspoon black pepper
 ¼ teaspoon cayenne powder
    vegetable oil for deep-frying

Batter

  1 cup flour
  1 cup water
  2 tablespoons vegetable oil or melted butter
  1 teaspoon salt
    dash of sugar (optional)
  1 egg (optional—if not using add ¼ cup extra water)

- Soak fish at least 8 hours in several changes of cold water. Drain and place in pan with water to cover. Bring to boil, reduce heat and simmer 5 minutes. Remove from heat and let stand for 20 minutes.
- Peel and quarter potatoes. Place in pan with water to cover. Bring to boil and cook about 15 minutes, or until tender when pierced with knife. Drain well, add milk and butter and mash well. Do not whip.
- Drain fish and flake with fork. Add 2½ cups potatoes (eat any leftovers) and mix well. Beat in eggs, one at a time, and mix in spices.
- Prepare the batter by beating together all ingredients, eliminating lumps. Let sit, covered, about 20 minutes.
- Form cod mixture into balls no larger than ¾ inch in diameter. Dip into batter and fry, about 6 at a time, in 3 inches of oil heated to 375°. Drain on paper towels.

● ●

CAESAR SALAD
WITH
FRIED OYSTERS

We have nothing against croutons, dear little garlic-and-oil sponges that they are (as you'll see, we make our own), but when a friend in New Hampshire served us a Caesar salad in which the croutons were replaced with fried oysters, we knew we had run into another splendidly gilded lily. The funny thing is, a lot of people hear about this recipe and say, "Oh, that's a meal in itself." It is not a meal in itself. It's a nice first course when you're having a boned, stuffed leg of lamb.

Oysters
   2 eggs
   2 tablespoons water
   2 dozen oysters, shucked
   1 cup fine bread crumbs, seasoned with salt and pepper
      peanut or vegetable oil for frying

Salad
   2 large or three medium heads chilled romaine lettuce
   ⅓ cup olive oil with 3 cloves crushed garlic, allowed to stand
      for 6 hours
   3 tablespoons wine vinegar
      juice of 1 lemon
   2 eggs, coddled 1 minute
   ¼ teaspoon Worcestershire sauce
      salt and freshly ground black pepper
   ½ cup grated Parmesan

- To prepare oysters for frying, blend eggs and water thoroughly. Dip each oyster separately in egg mixture, then roll in crumbs. Set aside on plate for ½ hour.
- To make the salad, remove and discard coarse outer leaves of romaine, tear lettuce into 2- to 3-inch pieces, and place in bowl.
- To fry the oysters, heat peanut oil over medium-high heat; do not allow to smoke. Fry oysters until golden, turning once. Do not overcook or they will be tough. Drain on paper towels.
- While oysters are frying, add olive oil (discard garlic), vinegar, and lemon juice to lettuce; break in eggs and toss. Season with Worcestershire, salt, and plenty of freshly ground black pepper. Add cheese and toss again until well mixed (all of the lettuce pieces should be nicely coated with dressing). Divide salad into 4 individual plates or shallow bowls, and garnish each plate or bowl with 6 fried oysters.

● ●

DEEP-FRIED SQUID/CUTTLEFISH

Here's a good example of marrying the batter to the food. Thin rings of squid need the batter only to protect their delicate flesh; they're light enough that tons of batter would only mask their taste and texture.

If you can find cuttlefish, so much the better; their flesh is both thicker and sweeter than squid. They are generally found only in good Italian, Portuguese, or Greek fish markets. If they're frozen, buy them anyway—it doesn't seem to have any effect on the flesh. When asking for them keep in mind the last five hundred years of art history, specifically the wealth of drawings done in sepia ink and wash. A good mnemonic device is Giovanni Domenico Tiepolo—think of him and you'll remember to ask for seppie. *Otherwise, no one will know what you're talking about.*

2 pounds cleaned squid or cuttlefish ("*seppie*")
1½ cups flour
1½ cups dry white wine
    salt and pepper
    cayenne pepper
    fat for deep-frying
    fresh-squeezed lemon juice

- If using squid, cut bodies into ¼-inch rings; if using cuttlefish, cut bodies into strips about ⅜ inch by 2 inches. Rinse and pat dry.
- Make batter by mixing flour and wine to make a thin mixture. If too thin it won't hold up to the fat; if too thick you'll get doughy squid. Add salt and pepper to taste and a dash of cayenne.
- Heat oil to 375° in deep fryer or heavy pot. A few at a time, dip pieces in batter, let excess drip off, then add to fat. Cook until golden. Drain on paper towels and sprinkle with lemon juice and salt.

● ●

FRIED CHICKEN

Trying to figure out the "best" way to fry chicken is like making your cat nervous by picking up a skinning knife: there are lots of ways to do it and everybody's an expert. Some folks say get a lean bird and some say fat; they'll argue about how much butter or lard or bacon fat to fry in; they'll go to the barricades over using batter or plain flour.

We agree with Ms. Antoinette: let them eat cake, or in this case, chicken. This is a good recipe. If you don't like it, try a different one.

> frying chickens
> milk
> salt and pepper
> flour
> fat

- Cut chickens into serving pieces. Soak at least 4 hours in milk. Dry thoroughly and sprinkle with salt and pepper. Dredge with flour and more salt and pepper; shake to coat all pieces well. Don't crowd the bag.
- Put enough fat in cast iron skillet to reach depth of ½ inch; heat until hot but not smoking. Gently lay chicken pieces in fat, being careful not to crowd them. Cook until golden brown on bottom; turn and repeat. Total cooking time should be about 20 minutes, slightly more for dark meat.

• •

PAPER BAG FRIED CHICKEN

See, what did we tell you? No sooner than one expert tells you how to fry chicken, another country is heard from. Go figure.

1 cup flour
2 tablespoons baking powder
  salt and pepper
1 chicken, cut up in frying pieces
  fat of choice

- Mix together flour, baking powder, and salt and pepper. Put in lunch-size paper bag. Add chicken pieces, 3 at a time. Hold top of bag shut tightly and shake like hell until pieces are well coated. Shake to remove excess flour.
- Heat about 1 inch fat in heavy skillet. Add chicken and fry until cooked.

● ●

ROESTI CREAM POTATOES

It's time again to gild the lilies. Why mess with a classic like roesti potatoes? The only real reason is that we also like cheese and heavy cream, and had them on hand as dinnertime neared.

Most roesti recipes call for parboiling the potatoes; it's not really necessary in this version because of the liquid in the heavy cream. What we save in cooking time we make up in friendly fat. The key is cooking at a heat high enough to brown the bottom, but low enough to permit a fairly lengthy cooking time for what is actually no more than a potato pancake. When done properly, the result is two thin discs of extremely crunchy potatoes held together by potato puree completely infused by butterfat. When was the last time you had potatoes drip down your chin?

4 medium potatoes
4 tablespoons butter
½ cup heavy cream
　salt and pepper
½ cup grated Gruyère (optional)

- Using large holes of a grater, shred potatoes; soak in cold water for 5 minutes. Drain well and pat dry with towel.
- Melt 2 tablespoons of the butter in a nonstick skillet. When foam begins to subside, add potatoes, pressing down with spatula to form cake. After 5 minutes, the bottom should start to brown slightly. Dribble cream onto potatoes, working in a spiral toward the outside edge. Add salt and pepper to taste. Turn heat up slightly to reduce cream, shaking pan frequently to prevent sticking.
- When bottom is well browned, flip as follows: Place buttered flat plate or cookie sheet over skillet; invert cake onto plate. Add remaining 2 tablespoons butter to skillet, melt, then carefully slide cake, uncooked-side down, into skillet. Continue cooking and shaking occasionally, until bottom is also well browned, about 15 minutes. If desired, sprinkle Gruyère evenly over surface about 5 minutes before done. Invert onto serving platter.

● ●

FATGATE, OR, OLEOMARGARINE COMES TO WISCONSIN

Bedtime reading sometimes makes for strange dreams. We were recently browsing through the *Laws of Wisconsin, 1931* and came across some pretty incendiary rantings in Chapter 96, subsection 98.39; laws beginning with "No person shall . . ." have always made us very nervous. Anyway:

"NO PERSON SHALL BY HIMSELF, OR BY HIS SERVANT OR AGENT, MANUFACTURE, SELL, EXCHANGE, OFFER OR EXPOSE FOR SALE, HAVE IN POSSESSION WITH INTENT TO SELL, OR SERVE TO GUESTS OR PATRONS FOR COMPENSATION IN A HOTEL, RESTAURANT OR BOARDING HOUSE . . ."

This is strong stuff; we expected folks to be in an uproar over a spate of poisoned Chiclets or Chinese restaurants doing a brisk back-door trade in spare cats; we thought of Baptist preachers drooling and raving over the curse of demon rum, stopping only to take a draw on the cough medicine. But let's get back to the law.

" . . . ANY OLEOMARGARINE, BUTTERINE, OR SIMILAR SUBSTANCE, WITHOUT FIRST SECURING A LICENSE FROM THE DEPARTMENT OF AGRICULTURE AND MARKETS."

Geez.
Oleomargarine? Butterine?

"EVERY LICENSED . . . SHALL KEEP A RECORD OF EVERY SALE AND SHIPMENT . . . PERSON TO WHOM . . . PLACE TO WHICH . . . TRANSPORTATION COMPANY . . . STATING THE DATE . . . ALL PURCHASES . . . SHALL MAKE A REPORT . . . TEN DAYS AFTER . . . SETTING FORTH . . . FAILURE . . . SUCH REPORTS . . . CAUSE . . . REVOCATION."

Granted, American legislators have always prided themselves on saving people from various instruments of destruction. We were, after all, the only Western nation to bar thalidomide in the sixties; sale of liquor and other drugs has usually been heavily regulated and taxed. You can't just walk over to the nearest Walgreens and pick up a vial of morphine; in states such as North Carolina you have to be old enough to reach over the counter to buy a pack of unfiltered Camels. Indeed, awash in a sea of departments and rules, about the only things you can pick up anywhere in America are harmless toys and powders like Uzis and AK-47s, angel dust and crack. But margarine? What were Nitschke, Gehrmann, Schroeder, Schwefel, and the other Wisconsin legislators of 1931 thinking?

The answer is simple: Wisconsin grows milch cows, which make milk, which people with names like Nitschke, Gehrmann, Schroeder, and Schwefel turn into butter. It's called protectionism and it's an old custom. In 1935 the oleo *tax* was 15 cents per pound; butter then sold for 36 cents per pound. For a second offense, a person putting unauthorized margarine on his macaroni could conceivably get, besides a lower cholesterol count, up to a year in the slammer and a thousand-dollar fine. They'd probably send him to a work farm and make him milk cows.

And this is all over the uncolored margarine, which looks like melted lard on your mashed potatoes. Until July 1, 1967, colored margarine could not be sold in the great state of Wisconsin. The state legislators made fools of themselves by passing joint resolutions asking the federal government to stop using butter substitutes in its welfare programs, and by exempting all the processed junk that gives cheese a bad name, as long as it was made of milk solids (1943). They forced manufacturers to put tax stamps on the margarine boxes (1949). In 1967 they dropped the tax on uncolored margarine but retained it for the colored. It's like reading a history of the poll tax in Georgia or Mississippi.

Finally, forty-two desperate years after the silliness started, the tax was repealed, ending family outings like bootleg margarine runs to Illinois or Minnesota. On December 31, 1973, margarine got cheap again. In the last five years of the law's life, per capita butter consumption in Wisconsin had fallen from 5.5 pounds to 5, while margarine consumption rose from 11 to 11.5 pounds. At the time of its death, the tax accounted for 10 to 31 percent of the price of a pound of oleo. Times change: Tail Gunner Joe was dead, and Wisconsin was off its gold standard.

●

PUFFED POTATOES WITH PÂTE-A-CHOUX

We include this recipe not only because it's good, but because it amounts to a very high-rent way to recreate a frozen-food-department favorite. Yes, this is how you make Tater Tots at home. Beyond that there's not much we can say about a side dish already known to all, except to remind you that due to the presence of a light, airy pastry mixture in this recipe, you will have to eat twice as many of these *in order to achieve the same sense of inner peace as you would from half a pound of french fries.*

Pâte

  ½ teaspoon salt
  6 tablespoons butter
  2 cups sifted flour
  8 eggs

Potatoes

2½ pounds boiling potatoes
10 tablespoons butter
  1 whole egg
  3 egg yolks
     salt and pepper
     nutmeg
     olive oil for frying

- To make pâte, bring 2 cups cold water to boil, along with the salt and butter. Remove from heat and add the flour all at once. Stir until well mixed and return to medium heat, stirring constantly until mixture gathers around spoon and pulls away from pan sides. Remove from heat and add the eggs, one at a time, stirring well after each addition.
- Peel potatoes, cut in quarters, and bring to boil. Cook until tender. Drain well and put through potato ricer. Add butter and stir until melted. Beat egg and yolks together and add gradually, stirring well. Add salt, pepper, and dash of nutmeg.
- Mix potato and pâte-a-choux dough until very well combined. Put mixture in pastry bag fitted with large star tube. Hold over large frying pan with 1 inch very hot olive oil. Squeeze mixture into oil, cutting off at 2-inch intervals. Fry until golden brown.

• •

POTATO CROQUETTES

These used to be a Sunday dinner fixture for he who grew up in Jersey. It's hard to recall just what they used to accompany; the strongest recollections they summon are not of their companion dishes, but of the whole gestalt of a Sunday night in Paterson. Invariably, during dinner, GE College Bowl *would be on, so we could "match wits with the champions" while sucking down potato croquettes. Allen Ludden would ask, "Who was Louis the Fourteenth's Finance Minister?" and we'd blurt out, "Ghlfberphft!" And Colbert it was. On a really good Sunday night, not only would Mom have made potato croquettes, but Ed Sullivan would have The Supremes on, so that we could wax concupiscent over Diana Ross while allowing the full enormity of what we'd done at table to settle into our gullet. Diana was a mystery, but at least we knew we could handle nine potato croquettes.*

      6 Idaho potatoes
      2 egg yolks
      4 tablespoons butter
      I cup flour
      2 whole eggs, beaten
         bread crumbs
    ½ cup Italian parsley, minced
         salt and pepper
         olive oil

- Peel and boil the potatoes. When tender, put through a ricer, add egg yolks and butter, and whip. Cool and form into 4-inch logs. Dip in flour, then beaten eggs, then in bread crumbs mixed with the parsley, salt, and pepper. Fry in olive oil until golden.

● ●

CHAPTER 5

ETHNIC HEAVYWEIGHTS

W E'VE ALWAYS LIKED the idea of the commemorative wall at Ellis Island, where if you send in a hundred dollars, they put the name of the immigrant ancestor of your choice on a public roster of honor. We realize that most of the immigrant ancestors in question would have thought this was a pretty nutty thing to do with a hundred bucks, which in their day would have bought the answers to the police exam, but after years of making a fuss over Plymouth Rock it's nice to see America honoring people who were welcomed to these shores by the Public Health Department rather than the Massachusetts Indians.

But we'd like to go the Ellis Island foundation one better. Instead of simply entitling you to put Grandma Facigaluppi's name on a wall, your hundred-dollar contribution (half of which goes to us, because we thought this up) buys you a spot in a public-access computer bank for your ethnic family's favorite recipe. Think of it—you'd take the shuttle boat out to Ellis Island, see the buildings and exhibits, and then queue up for your allotted minutes at a monitor, keyboard, and printer. It would work like the computerized card file in a high-tech library, only instead of entering in author or subject or title, you'd enter in nationality and main ingredient. In a matter of seconds, you'd know what Serbians did with eggplants, or what Poles made when the carp were running. Or, you could punch in a generic recipe title—say, "spaghetti sauce"—and scroll through hundreds of recipes. They could even be annotated: Imagine how touching it would be to get to the end of a recipe and read, "Stan liked these when his friends came over to play cards," or "Grandma used to carry this to Uncle Emil in a bucket when he worked in the slag drains at Bethlehem Steel."

Probably no one will pick up on this idea, but it's our way of reminding you that the greatest glory of American cuisine lies in its hearty, satisfying recipes brought here by people who arrived in boats that were not made of wood. And if your ancestors were greeted by Massasoit, put down that forkful of boiled cod and read up.

● ●

PORTUGUESE KALE SOUP

We found this recipe in an old book in the library of a famous American painter, whose Cape Cod house we rented one summer back in the late 1970s. We made the soup, and it turned out just like the version we loved at Cookie's in Provincetown. Cookie's is gone now, replaced by a yuppie ice cream shop: gone are the tourists, artists, and Portuguese fishermen lingering over their wonderful squid stew, vinegar-marinated haddock, and bowls of fava beans that you ate with a toothpick while the Red Sox blew another pennant on the TV at the bar.

    1 pound dry white beans—navy beans are good
    2 pounds fresh kale, washed and coarsely chopped
    1 pound linguiça sausage
    5 or 6 potatoes, thickly sliced
       salt and pepper

● Wash the beans and boil them in 4 or 5 quarts of water for an hour, or until tender. Add the kale, washed and chopped coarsely, the linguica, and the potatoes. Season with salt and pepper. Add more water to cover all ingredients if necessary. Simmer gently for another hour.

● ●

MACARONI PIE

Another recipe from Grandma—the one in Paterson, not Woonsocket. Although the name "macaroni pie" has stuck over the years, this is actually best made with angel hair pasta, or capellini. This more traditional term means "little hairs," and has nothing to do with angels.

- ¼ pound *capellini*, or angel hair pasta
- 6 eggs
- ¼ pound prosciutto, diced
- ¼ pound mozzarella, diced
  freshly ground black pepper
- 1 tablespoon chopped parsley (optional)
- 3 tablespoons olive oil
- 3 tablespoons butter

- Cook noodles al dente; do not overcook. Rinse with cold water and drain. Beat eggs, adding prosciutto and mozzarella. Season with black pepper and parsley, if desired. Do not add salt; the prosciutto has enough already. Mix in the cooked pasta.
- Heat 2 tablespoons each oil and butter in a nonstick frying pan. When hot, add noodle mixture. Cook on medium heat until bottom is lightly browned and crusty; remove from heat. Cover with a large plate (make sure bottom is loose before you do this), turn onto plate, scrape any loose particles from pan, add remaining 1 tablespoon each butter and oil to the pan, and slide pie back into pan. When pie feels firm to the touch and the bottom is lightly browned, remove from pan. May be eaten warm or cold.

● ●

MEATBALL, POTATO, AND STRING BEAN STEW IN TOMATO SAUCE

Over the river (the Passaic) and through what must have once been woods, to Grandmother's house we go. When we get there, Grandmother will have a dish like this one simmering on the stove—the one that looks like a '48 Buick, down in the basement, not the one she bought for show in 1964 and only boils water on.

2 slices stale bread, soaked in a little milk, then squeezed dry
1 large egg
1 pound lean ground beef
1 teaspoon chopped parsley
1 clove garlic, minced
2 teaspoons salt
  freshly ground black pepper
½ cup fine dry bread crumbs
1 small onion, diced
½ cup olive oil
3 large Idaho potatoes
½ pound fresh string beans, cut into 1-inch pieces
1 large can Italian plum tomatoes
1 teaspoon oregano
½ cup dry red wine

- To prepare the meatballs, mix soaked bread, egg, ground beef, parsley, garlic, 1 teaspoon of the salt, and pepper and form into balls. Roll in bread crumbs. Sauté diced onion in ¼ cup of the olive oil and add meatballs, turning until browned, but not cooked through. Remove onions and meatballs with slotted spoon and set aside.
- Slice potatoes lengthwise into thick slices, add remaining ¼ cup olive oil to skillet and heat. When oil is hot, fry potatoes, browning slightly but not completely cooking through. Remove and reserve.
- Boil or steam string beans for several minutes and drain.
- In a large saucepan, place meatballs, onions, potatoes, and string beans. Pour in tomatoes (strained or unstrained, as you prefer). Add remaining 1 teaspoon salt, pepper, and oregano and simmer over medium heat for an hour. Ten minutes before completion, add wine and bring to a boil. (If liquid cooks down too much during simmering, add a little beef broth.)

• •

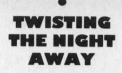

TWISTING
THE NIGHT
AWAY

About ten years ago, we noticed a strange trend in recipes in cookbooks and newspapers: cooks started telling us exactly how many times we should twist our peppermill. At first we wrote this off as one more sop to those all-time consumers of things thought exclusive and special, yuppies. After all, it assumes that the reader *has* a peppermill; its precision appeals to a group that has given up rational thought and differentiation. As long as they're sure that they're doing *exactly the right thing,* the kids are happy on the one night a month they're not eating out.

The only problem is, counting "twists" is as precise as saying "have enough drinks to relax." We know a few people who have been counting the coasters for close to a lifetime, and they're a lot closer to rigor mortis than they are to relaxation. So, once again in the interest of scientific inquiry, we've checked it out for you. The obvious moral is: grind enough pepper to make yourself happy.

Tests were conducted as follows: grinder was held upright on level surface over aluminum foil and handle or top rotated exactly ten 360° revolutions. Samples were weighed on electronic jewellers' scale reading to 1/1,000 carat and converted to ounces with Sanyo calculator.

RANK	SAMPLE (OUNCE)	REMARKS
1	.04229	"Garantic Spade," whatever that means. Made in Italy.
2	.02355	Chrome crank-type, "A Maison Product" from Taiwan.
3	.01858	Steel Perfex, made in France. An industrial-strength tool.
4	.01482	Ceramic, made in Japan. Broke immediately after test.
5	.01366	6 inches tall, Lucite, looks like half of the World Trade Center.
6	.01062	12 inches high, teak, in shape of chess king.
7	.01035	Cole & Mason #505, acrylic plastic. "A gift from Mom."
8	.01007	"Grinder #1," set to coarse. Labeling on adjuster ring is backwards.
9	.00894	Small plastic throwaway, 1½-inch diameter, 2 inches high.
10	.00821	"Olde Thompson," Sheffield works, found in trendy New York café.
11	.00647	21 inches high, ground by a waiter named Rick. Size isn't everything (see Hemingway/Fitzgerald, page 20).
12	.0061	Brass, made in Greece, says "GUAPAN EE."
13	.005	"Rita," by Le Mill, #3700 salt and pepper combo. Invented by Bill Bounds.
14	.00436	Rick again. 10 inches high, 2½-inch diameter.
15	.00334	Generic grinder, found in New Jersey. No identifying marks.
16	.00287	Rick gives number 14 a second try.
17	.00252	Another Bill Bounds. Twenty-five-year guarantee (no wonder, with such a measly output!).

●

PIZZA PIENA (ITALIAN EASTER PIE)

In northern New Jersey, the greeting most commonly heard during the last few days before Easter is not "Happy Easter" or even "Buona Pasqua," but "Did you get your pies done yet?" Under the circumstances, North Jersey's ethnic fiber being what it is, the pie in question is Pizza Piena, literally "full pie." And a full pie it is. We've heard non-Italians describe it as a sort of giant quiche, but that's like comparing a New Orleans Po' Boy to a finger sandwich at high tea. And unlike quiche, Easter Pie is a dish for all meals—an entire breakfast, lunch, or dinner in a crust, delicious hot or cold. So join us in our memories of those Holy Saturdays of yesteryear, when the only thing a Jersey boy looked forward to more than fresh-from-the-oven Easter Pie was the giant chocolate crucifix he was sure the Bunny was going to bring the following morning.

Crust

   2 teaspoons salt
     black pepper (optional)
   7 cups flour
1½ cups butter, chilled and cut in pieces
   ¾ cups lard
   8 egg yolks plus enough ice water to equal 2 cups

Filling

- 1 pound soprassata (coarse, cured Italian salami-like sausage), skin removed and diced
- 1 pound prosciutto, diced
- 1½ pounds mozzarella, sliced or diced
- 1½ pounds fresh ricotta (sold in Italian markets as "basket cheese"), cut into slices
- 6 hard-boiled eggs, sliced
- 1 dozen eggs
- ½ gallon milk
  freshly ground black pepper
- 1 egg yolk mixed with 2 tablespoons water, for brushing

- To make the crust, sift salt and pepper, if using, into the flour, and work in the butter and lard (fingers are best for this job). Add the egg-water mixture, stirring until it forms a ball. The dough should be soft, but not sticky. A little more flour may be added if necessary. Refrigerate for several hours or overnight.

- Roll out half of the dough and line 6 9-inch pie or cake pans, leaving a little overhang. Set oven at 350°.

- Fill pastry-lined pans half full with soprassata, prosciutto, mozzarella, ricotta, and sliced eggs. Beat eggs with milk, adding black pepper to taste. Pour this mixture over ingredients in pans, filling to within ½ inch of top. Roll out remaining dough and cover each pan, sealing edges tightly. Make several slashes in top for steam to escape. (If you have dough left over, you can use it to decorate the tops. For Easter, a cross is traditional.) Brush with egg-water wash and bake for 40 minutes or until crust is nicely browned. Allow to cool slightly before cutting, so the filling can set. If you use a deeper pan, increase baking time to 1 hour.

● ●

• •

EGGPLANT WITH PASTA AND PORK AND OIL

We started this one off as an essay in healthful substitution. It's basically a lasagna, with a few changes. Since, according to some warped views, carbohydrates are undesirable, we changed the noodles to eggplant slices. So far, so good, sort of.

Then we were going to replace the cheese with eggplant too but not only was the color wrong but the slices had soaked up so much oil that the no-no inspection team would whack our knuckles. So we said, what the hell, it's a lost cause and threw in some pork, heavy cream, elbow pasta, and lots of Parmesan.

Probably the lesson here is a combination of "you can't always get what you want" and "you can't please everyone, so you've got to please yourself." It all boils down to "You can't fool all the people . . ." so why try?

3	medium eggplants, about 3 pounds total
2	cloves garlic
12	tablespoons good olive oil, or more as necessary
1½	pounds ground lean pork
1	35-ounce can crushed tomatoes
2	teaspoons basil
	salt and pepper
1	cup heavy cream
1	pound short pasta, such as elbows or penne
1	large red onion
½	cup grated Parmesan
2	tablespoons butter

- Cut eggplant into ⅜-inch slices. Sprinkle both sides with salt and set aside for 30 minutes. Mince garlic and cook slowly, without browning, in 2 tablespoons of the oil for 5 minutes. Add pork and sauté until pink color disappears. Break up meat clumps. Add tomatoes, basil, and salt and pepper to taste and simmer 45 minutes. Add cream, stir to mix well and remove from heat.
- Bring large quantity of water to boil and cook pasta until almost done, about 7 to 12 minutes depending on brand. Drain and place in large bowl of cold water.
- Blot eggplant slices with paper towels to remove salt and moisture that has gathered on surface. Heat 8 tablespoons of the olive oil and sauté eggplant slices until golden and soft. They will soak up huge amounts of oil but will release it as cooking progresses. Do not crowd pan. Additional oil may be necessary.
- Finely chop the onion and cook slowly in remaining 2 table-spoons oil until soft.
- Assemble dish by putting a few spoons of tomato sauce into bottom of oiled large baking dish. Add a layer of drained pasta, sprinkle with onions and a layer of sauce. Cover with eggplant slices. Repeat until pan is filled. Finish with eggplant topped with sauce. Sprinkle with Parmesan, dot with butter, and bake 45 minutes at 375°, or until top is browned and casserole bubbles vigorously. Let stand 15 minutes before serving.

● ●

EGGPLANT PARMESAN

A dish about which little has to be said, and about which everything is right. It's got presence, it's got heft, it's got to-mato sauce, it's got olive oil, and you can make sandwiches out of it. But here's a little-known fact: if you assemble this dish up to the point where it goes into the oven and then freeze it before baking, the eggplant will get smoother and creamier. Don't thaw before baking; just pop it into a 350° oven (no microwaves) for an hour or until it's heated through and the cheese is browned.

    1 large eggplant, peeled and sliced in ¼- to ½-inch slices
    ⅔ cup flour
    2 eggs, beaten
    ⅔ cup fine bread crumbs
      olive oil for frying
    3 to 4 cups of your favorite tomato sauce, with or without
        meat (We prefer meat sauce; see our recipe, page 110)
    1 pound sliced mozzarella, fresh if you can get it
    ½ cup grated Parmesan

- Dredge eggplant slices in flour, dip in egg, and coat with bread crumbs. Fry breaded slices in olive oil until they are dark golden and offer little resistance to a fork. Drain on paper towels.
- In a 9-by-12-by-3-inch casserole, spoon a thin layer of tomato sauce over the bottom. Put down a single layer of fried eggplant slices, followed by a generous layer of sauce, moz-zarella slices, and a sprinkling of Parmesan. Continue repeat-ing process until eggplant and mozzarella are used up (you'll probably get 2 layers of eggplant), ending with a final layer of sliced mozzarella on top. Bake in a 350° oven for 40 minutes, making sure that cheese on top is melted and browned nicely. You can use the broiler for browning during the last few minutes, but don't overdo it.

● ●

MIDDLE EASTERN EGGPLANT AND CHICK-PEA CASSEROLE

We've come across this dish in several Middle Eastern cookbooks, but we wonder if it's really a part of the Arab repertoire. It doesn't matter; it tastes good, especially served at room temperature in a pita pocket. Have a napkin handy; never will you see so much oil drip down your chin. It's easier if you eat it with two hands, but we are not recommending that because we don't want to live in a broom closet under assumed names for the rest of our lives.

> 1 cup dried chick-peas
> 2 large onions, peeled and cut in ¼-inch slices
> ⅔ cup olive oil, more as necessary
> 1 large eggplant, peeled and cut in ¾-inch cubes
> 1 large can Italian tomatoes, drained and coarsely chopped
>   salt and pepper

- Soak chick-peas for 3 hours. Boil in plenty of unsalted water for 1 hour, or until barely tender. Drain and reserve.
- In a large oven-proof/stovetop casserole, sauté sliced onions in a few tablespoons of the olive oil until soft and golden; do not brown. Set onions aside, and add ⅓ cup olive oil to pan. When oil is hot, begin sautéing eggplant cubes in batches, removing with a slotted spoon when soft and barely beginning to brown. Add the rest of the oil as you sauté remaining eggplant; use more oil if necessary. When all eggplant is done, drain excess oil from pot, and add eggplant, sautéed onions, cooked chick-peas, and tomatoes; season with salt and pepper to taste. Bring to a boil on stove top, then place, covered, in 325° oven to continue cooking for 1 to 1½ hours, or until chick-peas are tender. Allow to cool nearly to room temperature before serving. If you refrigerate the leftovers, allow to *rise* to room temperature before serving.

● ●

CHOUCROUTE GARNIE

Back in 1976, we—meaning one of us and an erstwhile spouse—were motoring through Alsace-Lorraine, along the Route des Cretes. It was our singular misfortune to be traveling with an English couple so bereft of culinary sensibility that they had actually packed a giant lunch with which to tour France—an English lunch, complete with English margarine, that lasted them for days. It was then that it occurred to us that the reason these people conquered the world was that while waiting for relief from a siege, they could eat plumbing fixtures. Anyway, we finally talked these two into stopping at a restaurant—a little homey roadside place high up in the Vosges, specializing in the decidedly un-French cuisine of a region that, after all, gets to call itself Der Elsass *every few decades. The specialty of the house was the schizophrenically named* choucroute garnie, *not French exactly, as you'll see from the ingredients, but the kind of thing an Alsatian keeps simmering on the back burner in case any, ah, jack-booted guests show up for a late snack. It's the kind of dish* Mutter *used to make, a dish that would stick to your ribs all the way to Paris.*

½ pound slab bacon, preferably double-smoked, cut into 6 pieces

2 pounds pork spareribs, divided into 3 or 4 racks

2 pounds fresh sauerkraut (available in bulk from German delicatessens in large cities) or canned imported German sauerkraut

1 medium boiling potato, grated

½ teaspoon caraway seeds

1 bauernwurst (German ring sausage), about 12 inches

6 to 8 bratwurst or weisswurst

½ cup dry white wine

8 to 10 medium boiling potatoes, halved

- Place the bacon pieces in a heavy Dutch oven large enough to hold all ingredients. Fry bacon over medium heat until about 3 tablespoons fat have been rendered. Remove bacon and set aside; turn heat to medium-high, and brown spareribs.
- When spareribs are browned, turn heat to medium-low and add sauerkraut, grated potato, caraway seeds, sausages, and white wine. (Note: If you prefer, sausages can also be browned in advance.) Add reserved bacon pieces, and cook for 1½ hours, reducing heat to low. Cover while cooking.
- While sauerkraut and meats are simmering, parboil potatoes. One half hour before dish is finished cooking, add parboiled potatoes and cover again.
- To serve, heap sauerkraut onto large oval platter; surround with potatoes, and arrange meats artfully over and around kraut. Serve with dark rye bread (reserve juice for dipping!) and plenty of German (or Alsatian) beer.

PASTA WITH POTATOES AND CHEESE

Friends have always mocked us when we slip into reveries of cooking various kinds of pasta with potato. "You guys have really gone too far this time." Never ones to take a short hike when a long one is available, we've always taken this as a compliment.

We also enjoy putting complements together. If you consider that anything good with pasta is usually good with potatoes, why not save your energy and put them together at the outset? No one complains about sole stuffed with crabmeat, or calves' liver wrapped in bacon, or tournedos topped with foie gras.

If you replaced surf 'n' turf with potatoes 'n' pasta, restaurant food would be a lot more interesting and we'd all save a lot of money. And think of the health benefits: potatoes are not sea-bottom scavengers, and semolina wheat doesn't get fattened on steroids.

    1¼ pounds potatoes
     1 pound short pasta, such as penne or elbows
     3 tablespoons butter
     1 cup heavy cream
    ¼ pound feta cheese, grated
     1 tablespoon oregano
    ½ teaspoon black pepper
    ¼ teaspoon hot pepper flakes

- Peel potatoes and cut in ½-inch dice. Place in pan with water to cover and boil until just tender, 10 minutes or less.
- Meanwhile, bring large pot of water to boil and cook pasta to desired firmness. While pasta is cooking, melt butter in large skillet. Add cream, feta, and spices and bring to simmer. Add potatoes and cook long enough for them to heat through.

• Drain pasta and add to skillet. Turn heat to high and cook briefly (no more than 2 minutes), stirring constantly, then serve.

• •

STUFFED CABBAGE

Ah, Milwaukee,
Oh, Gdansk!
For pigs and cabbage
We give thanks.

Not that many people are aware of a lesser example of the Triangle Trade, coming considerably later than the Golden Age of New England. Having nothing except triangulation to link it to the nefarious dealings in slaves, sugar, and demon rum, this collection of trade routes runs roughly between Eastern Europe and southern Wisconsin with a mandatory stop-off at the Hog Butcher of the World.

We were in Poland for the last Commie spring, in 1989. What time wasn't spent looking for good meals was spent losing weight. A lot of dishes, such as incredibly fatty pork shins, seemed to exist only as a foil for beer and vodka. Diners all too willingly explained that the spirits helped cut the fat. Most of the other dishes depended on noodle dough and potatoes, as befits a nation whose slang for "butcher shop" translates as "naked hooks."

Bring these necessarily inventive cooks to the land of plenty, and they blossom. Imagine an epiphany of hogs rooting next to a field of cabbages, or suddenly realizing that you can get good potatoes any day of the year. Imagine walking into a grocery store and seeing more meat in one gleaming case than you've seen in the last ten years combined. Stuffed cabbage is one of the reasons we don't tell Polish jokes.

Sauce

    2   cloves garlic, minced
    2   tablespoons olive oil
    1   35-ounce can Italian tomatoes
    1   small can tomato paste
    8   ounces beef stock
    2   teaspoons basil
        salt and pepper

Cabbage

    1   pound ground pork
    1   pound sweet Italian sausage (must have fennel)
    1   medium yellow onion
    2   cloves garlic
    3   tablespoons butter
    1   cup raw rice
    2   cups beef stock
        salt and pepper
    2   teaspoons oregano
        red pepper flakes
    1   medium green cabbage
 1½   pounds bacon (optional)
    ¾   cup sour cream

- To prepare the sauce, gently sauté garlic in oil until soft but not browned, about 5 minutes. Puree tomatoes in food mill or food processor, add to garlic along with paste, stock, basil, and salt and pepper. Bring to boil, reduce heat and simmer one-half hour.
- Sauté ground pork and sausage in skillet, breaking up mixture with spoon. When pink color disappears, remove from heat and let cool. Do not drain.
- Finely mince onion and garlic and sauté in 2 tablespoons of the butter until golden. Put in a large mixing bowl.

- Meanwhile, cook rice in beef stock until done; stir in remaining tablespoon butter and salt and pepper to taste. Add to mixing bowl, along with cooled meat and any juices in pan. Mix well, adding oregano, generous dash of red pepper flakes, and more salt and pepper. It should be on the spicy side.
- Bring a large quantity of water to boil. Cut out core of cabbage and discard tough outer leaves. Carefully remove whole inner leaves. Cabbage should yield about 16 leaves, depending on the cook's perception of what's tough and what's too small. Blanch leaves, a few at a time, being very careful not to break them, until wilted, no more than 2 minutes.
- Stuff by placing leaves, one at a time, on flat surface. Place dollop of meat mixture in center, then roll up, tucking ends in as you go. Secure with toothpicks. For added taste and richness, cook separated strips of bacon until limp. Wrap each cabbage roll with strips on bias before securing with toothpicks. Sauté lightly and very carefully, then proceed.
- Place rolls in one layer in large oven-proof/stovetop casserole. Cover with sauce, gently lifting rolls with spoon to allow sauce to flow beneath them. Bring to bubbling on stove, then place, covered, in 350° oven for 45 minutes.
- To serve, remove rolls with slotted spoon and arrange on heated platter. (Remove toothpicks!) Add sour cream to sauce in casserole and heat through. Spoon over rolls.

• •

EXCEEDINGLY GENEROUS NOODLE SAUCE

Like so many chop-it-up-and-put-it-in-the-pot dishes, pasta sauce is forgiving. If you can keep in mind a few ideas of what definitely does not go with what, you're on safe ground. In a sauce like this, no matter what you add to it, if it tastes good the odds are someone in the past has done the same thing and also didn't throw it out.

    2 pounds sweet Italian sausage
    2 pounds ground beef
 1¼ pounds fresh mushrooms
    4 large red onions
    7 large cloves garlic
 ½ cup olive oil
    2 28-ounce cans crushed tomatoes
    2 28-ounce cans whole peeled tomatoes
    2 ounces tomato paste
    3 tablespoons dried basil
    1 tablespoon oregano
       salt and pepper
    1 teaspoon hot pepper flakes
    3 large carrots, peeled; tops and tips removed
    2 cups heavy cream

- Remove casings from sausage and mix meat with ground beef. Place in large frying pan and cook over medium heat until pink disappears; break up large clumps as meat cooks. Remove meat with slotted spoon, reserving fat and juices, and put in large, heavy pot.
- Wipe and slice mushrooms. Add to fat and juices from meat and cook until wilted and juice has evaporated. Add to large pot.

- Chop onions and garlic; sauté in olive oil until limp but not browned. Add to large pot.
- Add crushed tomatoes to meat/vegetable pot. Drain juice from whole tomatoes into large pot, then chop tomatoes roughly and add to pot.
- Bring sauce to boil, then reduce to simmer. Add tomato paste and stir to thoroughly blend. Add spices and stir. Add carrots and simmer 2 hours, stirring frequently. If too thick add water sparingly. Remove carrots and mash finely with fork, return to pot. Add heavy cream and simmer 20 minutes more.
- Makes enough to sauce about 6 pounds pasta, just right for a light Italian lunch.

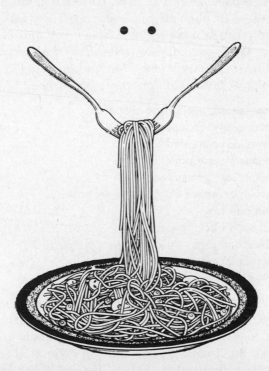

WOONSOCKET PORK PIE

Back near the beginning of the twentieth century, a couple of our grandparents moved south from the province of Quebec. Like so many French Canadians, they wound up working in the textile mills of New England. It wasn't that big a cultural leap: the weather was pretty much the same, maybe a bit warmer; they could still get pork and potatoes; and, if they moved to a city like Woonsocket, Rhode Island, everybody spoke French. The only real difference was that they now had jobs.

We've eaten tortiere *practically every Christmas since we were tall enough to blindly fling our hands up over the table's edge and grab whatever was there. If our left hand came down with a wedge of pork pie, we knew our right was probably pretty close to the bowl of cornichons, tiny sour-but-not-dill gherkins. As we got older we were allowed plates, and, later on, they trusted us with forks, but nothing else has changed, at least not as far as the pork pie is concerned.*

2 large onions, peeled and chopped
3 stalks celery, chopped
2 cloves garlic, minced
4 pounds ground pork
2 pounds lean ground beef
2 envelopes instant chicken or beef bouillon
1 teaspoon salt
1 teaspoon black pepper
1 tablespoon sage
1 cup fine bread crumbs
3 10-inch piecrusts, uncooked

• Add water to large pot to depth of 1 inch. Add onion, celery, and garlic to pot with ground meat and instant bouillon. Bring to boil and cook, covered, until meat is partially cooked. Stir frequently to break up clumps. Uncover and continue to simmer for total of 1 hour. Add salt and pepper and simmer for one-half hour. Add sage and simmer one-half hour. Remove from stove and cool. If there's an excess of fat, spoon off but do not remove all fat. Add bread crumbs and mix well.

- Divide among 3 pie shells and bake about 20 minutes at 400°. If desired, freeze uncooked.

• •

BREAD SOUFFLÉ

Bread soufflé is offered as an illustration of the effects of transatlantic travel on even the most basic foods; it's easier to write a recipe than it is to do a line drawing.

Something happened in America, between the invention of sliced white bread and the introduction of electric ranges, perhaps influenced by the Ladies' Home Journal *and cooking clubs. Italians have bread soup and bread salad, and make pasta sauce with bread crumbs and little else, and it's all wonderful; on this side of the pond, we get white bread soufflé.*

It could be worse. The future version will probably use Egg Beaters and skim milk.

    4 slices white bread
       butter
    I cup milk
    3 eggs
    2 cups grated sharp cheddar cheese
    ½ teaspoon dry mustard or I tablespoon Dijon mustard
       salt and pepper
       nutmeg

- Butter bread slices, trim off crusts, and cube. Spread in buttered baking dish, about 8 inches square. Mix all other ingredients and pour over bread cubes. Cover and let stand at least 8 hours. Bake 45 minutes at 325°.

CHOLENT

Cholent attempts a redefinition of "heavy food." After five hours in the oven the result is meat-flavored beans, meat-flavored potatoes, and bean-and-potato-flavored meat. One can distinguish the various elements by their general shape; the brisket's a little darker but not much. It's actually quite delicious, but definitely meant for cold weather in a cold climate; call a cardiologist before attempting it in August or it might be the last light in August you'll ever see.

This may be the right moment to dispel an age-old religious misconception. We've always assumed that the Sabbath observance led to so many Jewish recipes' being slow cookers in the oven; one could put it on a slow fire on Friday afternoon and have it reach a peak on Saturday without actually doing any work on the Sabbath. Actually, Russian Jews invented what has always been attributed to New England Yankees— bean-hole cooking. Cooking your cholent in a dirt-covered pot resting on hot stones, you could hide in the woods when you heard the cossacks thundering toward your village. When they left, you could grab your shovel and dig up a nice hot dinner.

1	pound dry beans (red or white kidney, lima, or any combination thereof)
¼	cup rendered chicken fat (see note below)
3	large yellow onions, peeled and sliced ⅛ inch thick
2	cloves garlic
3 to 4	pounds beef brisket or flank in 1 piece
2	tablespoons flour
2	teaspoons mild paprika
	salt and pepper
10	medium potatoes, peeled and quartered
1	large bay leaf

- Pick over beans and discard any small stones. Either soak beans overnight in cold water to cover or use the quick-and-dirty method: wash beans in cold water, put in saucepan with 5 cups water, and boil for a few minutes. Cover pan, remove from heat, and let stand an hour; proceed.
- Melt rendered fat in large oven-proof/stovetop casserole. Add onions and brown slightly over medium heat, separating rings with wooden spoon. Onions should be soft and golden brown. Remove onions with slotted spoon, reserving fat, and set aside.
- Meanwhile, cut garlic in slivers and stud meat all over. Mix the flour, paprika, and salt and pepper and sprinkle over meat, pressing with heel of hand. Be sure to coat meat evenly.
- Brown meat well over medium-high heat, adding more fat if necessary. Return onions to pot, along with the beans, the potatoes, and the bay leaf. Add boiling water to cover, about 6 cups.
- Bring to boil over high heat, cover tightly, and place in 300° oven. Leave undisturbed for 3 hours. Turn off oven (don't open door) and let pot sit for 2 more hours. Serve on large plates.

NOTE: *To make your own schmaltz (rendered chicken fat),* pull gobs of fat from any available chickens. Place in saucepan with cold water. Water should equal about ⅔ volume of fat. Place on low heat and let fat melt slowly but completely. When melted strain out any stray cracklings (shards of skin or flesh). Put water/fat in refrigerator. When fat has solidified, pry the cake out and wipe water from base. Fat will keep close to forever in refrigerator. This works with any animal fat you dare to render.

● ●

THE JAMES BEARD INDEX, or, Beancounting Time

•

THE BEST PART of writing cookbooks is doing the research. As some of our less-than-gracious friends have pointed out, we've been researching this one for eighty years now, and haven't we learned enough yet? The answer is, as always, don't throw us in that briar patch.

John F. Kennedy once remarked that the greatest assemblage of genius in the White House occurred when Thomas Jefferson dined alone; maybe so, but it must have been lonely. We hardly claim to be in Jefferson's class but we've always wondered what those meals were like. Did he just sit there and brood on the problems of a nascent democracy ? Maybe he figured out new ways to get his Bordeaux through customs without paying customs duty (we've tried that). Did he savor each morsel of country ham and backyard corn, or did he wait as the servants brought in course after course, giving him only enough time to slurp each entrée down before the next arrived?

The biggest problem about eating by yourself is that, obviously, there's no one there to share it with. The second biggest problem is what to do between bites, besides chewing. The usual technique has always been to take another bite; in many cases this leads to eight-minute meals or 250-pound bodies, or both. We've each had periodic practice as lonely guys, and have come up with a happy solution: we read cookbooks.

We've never believed in take-out, nor would we ever cook

dreck just because we're eating alone. However, there are limits; we're not about to spend eight hours cooking for one meal. So, prepare something simple but tasty, like a nice plate of *tagliatelle con dadi di prosciutto*, then go to your bookshelves and pick a guest. Dinner with Julia perhaps, or Sunday brunch with James Beard. Take M.F.K. Fisher to lunch, have a late-night snack with Brillat-Savarin. They're all literate, and some of them are lots better company than some folks we've mistakenly invited over. Plus, there aren't any permanent consequences, not to mention legal ones.

So, when we started checking out how others have dealt with the concept of heavy food, we knew where to look. One of the first things was to take down our old favorites and see how they stacked up. We've always tried our best to be precise, in some things at least (it gives us more slop room in the others), and we wondered how to codify or at least rank the books. The answer came, not as a salamander waving a golden plate around, but as the James Beard Index. As befits a man who seemed to have spent a good part of his life wiping butter off his chins, the JBI centers on cooking fats.

Like $E=mc^2$, the index is simplicity itself. First, go through every recipe in a given cookbook and add up every tablespoon of fat in the ingredients, and divide by the number of pages of recipes. The result is the James Beard Index for that book. Using only recipe pages allows us to disregard long-winded introductions, or page upon page of basic instructions: here is how we chop, here is how we slice, here is how we butterfly, now ain't that nice. When we came to a direction like "4 to 6 tablespoons or more butter," we took the literalist route: we went for the 6, but didn't skew the results by saying, what the hell, let's put in 14. Similarly, when a french-fry recipe called for "fat for deep-frying" we didn't add two quarts to the total, but when Paul Prudhomme said "add 3 sticks of margarine," we did, with pleasure. After all, we do believe in an ordered world.

The results were telling. Our champ, Buster Holmes, came from New Orleans, where the point of eating crayfish is not the meat (there isn't any) but sucking the fat from the shells. Similarly, an opportunist like Michel Guerard (how to get thin by spending a lot of money while underfeeding yourself) deserves last place, if only for having a recipe that calls for a teaspoon of fat. It takes more energy than that to wash the spoon. We're generous enough to think he won't mind coming in last; after all, his "spa," Les Prés d'Eugénie, probably took in more cash in a year than Buster Holmes did in his lifetime. (There was a lot more laughter at Buster's though, and that's why we ate there.)

The JBI says a lot about different cooks' attitudes toward food. If you exclude *Beard on Bread*, his six other books fall within a nine-place slot. Two of the others in that grouping, 5 through 13, are different editions of the same book, *Fannie Farmer*. Similarly, with four books on the chart, Julia Child lets only one other author cut into her line. We appreciate consistency and a well-thought-out moral code, and wouldn't have thought of it this way if we hadn't done the JBI. Knowledge is power, and fat helps the food slide down.

● ●

Rank	Title	Author	Year
1	The Buster Holmes Restaurant Cookbook[2]	Buster Holmes[3]	1983
2	American Charcuterie[5]	Victoria Wise[6]	1986
3	Chef Paul Prudhomme's Louisiana Kitchen[7]	Paul Prudhomme[8]	1984
4	Foie Gras, Magret, and Other Good Food from Gascony[10]	Andre Daguin, Anne de Ravel	1988
5	The New James Beard[11]	James Beard	1981
6	The Fannie Farmer Cookbook[14]	Marion Cunningham	1990
7	James Beard's Menus for Entertaining	James Beard	1965
8	James Beard's American Cookery[17]	James Beard[18]	1972
9	The Low Salt, Low Cholesterol Cookbook[21,22]	Myra Waldo	1961
10	The Fannie Farmer Cookbook[23]	Fannie Farmer	1912[24]
11	Beard on Pasta	James Beard[25]	1990
12	James Beard's New Fish Cookery[26]	James Beard	1954
13	James Beard's Theory and Practice of Good Cooking[27]	James Beard	1977
14	Mastering the Art of French Cooking[28]	J. Child, L. Bertholle, S. Beck	1961
15	From Julia Child's Kitchen	Julia Child[29]	1975
16	The Way to Cook[30]	Julia Child[31]	1989
17	The Best of British Cooking[34]	Marika Hamburg Tennison	1976
18	Mastering the Art of French Cooking, Volume II	Julia Child, Simone Beck[35]	1970
19	Manifold Destiny[36]	Chris Maynard, Bill Scheller[37]	1989[38]
20	Beard on Bread[40]	James Beard	1973
21	Pierre Franey's Low-Calorie Gourmet[42]	Pierre Franey	1984
12	Cuisine Minceur[44]	Michel Guerard[45]	1976

1 Using milking machine.
2 Only snap-on plastic binding in sample.
3 He died a happy man.
4 Second-place Even Cow award.
5 Uses directions like "6 cups rendered fat."
6 Lives in Berkeley!
7 Tartar and cranberry sauces use butter.
8 Writes instructions such as "add three sticks butter."
9 A full day's work.
10 Original in French.
11 Calls for veggie ratio of 2 pounds vegetables to 1 stick butter.
12 We like the symmetry of even numbers.

JBI	T fat	Ounces fat	Pounds fat	Cows milked	Quarts milk	Hours of milking[1]	Cubic feet of butter
8.37	862.5	431.25	27	60 [4]	1080	3.48	.456
6.97	1867	933.5	58.34	129.6	2333.2	7.5	.985
6.22	1989.4	994.7	62.17	138.1	2486.4	8 [9]	1.05
6.21	1106	553	34.5	76.7	1380	4.4	.583
5.96	3200.5	1600.25	100 [12]	222.2	4000 [13]	12.9	1.689
5.85	4368	2184	136.5	303.3	5460	17.6	2.306
5.71 [15]	2117.1	1058.5	66.17	147 [16]	2646.4	8.5	1.118
5.64	4803.3	2401.65	150.1 [19]	333.6	6004	19.3	2.535 [20]
4.67	910.5	455.25	28.5	63.3	1140	3.7	.481
3.72	1509	754.5	47.13	104.7	1884.8	6.1	.796
3.41	580	250	18.13	40.3	724.8	2.3	.306
3.37	1617.5	808.75	50.5	112.2	2020	6.5	.853
3.34	1249	624.5	39	86.7	1560	5	.659
2.99	1935	967.6	60.5	134.4	2420	7.8	1.022
2.90	1816	908	56.75	126.1	2270	7.3	1.009
2.83	1387.5 [32]	693.75	43.34	96.3	1733.2	5.6 [33]	.732
2.73	568	284	17.75	39.4	710	2.3	.3
2.68	1360.5	680.25	42.5	94.4	1700	5.5	.718
2.21	106	52 [39]	3.25	7.2	130	.4	.055
2.00	456.6 [41]	228.3	14.25	31.7	570	1.8	.241
1.95	489	244.5	15.3	34 [43]	612	2	.258
.42	98.45 [46]	49.25	3.08	6.8	123.2	.4 [47]	.052

13 Ditto.
14 Special symbols for vegetarian and microwave dishes.
15 Entertaining rather richly.
16 First place, Even Cow award.
17 A great book.
18 A large man.
19 The champ in tonnage.
20 Bigger than most small children.
21 Sexist, therefore politically incorrect.
22 Plus, boring.
23 An eponymous library book.
24 Also, oldest book.

Rank	Title	Sticks of butter	Calories from fat	Hours sleeping
1	The Buster Holmes Restaurant Cookbook	108	110,700	1703.1
2	American Charcuterie	233.32	239,153	3679.3
3	Chef Paul Prudhomme's Louisiana Kitchen	248.64	254,856	3920.9
4	Foie Gras, Magret, and Other Good Food from Gascony	138	141,450	2176.2
5	The New James Beard	400[52]	410,000[53]	6307.7
6	The Fannie Farmer Cookbook	546	559,650	8610
7	James Beard's Menus for Entertaining	264.64	271,256	4173.2
8	James Beard's American Cookery	600.4	615,410	9467.8
9	The Low Salt, Low Cholesterol Cookbook	114	116,850	1797.7
10	The Fannie Farmer Cookbook	188.5	193,192	2972.2
11	Beard on Pasta	72.5	74,292	1143[55]
12	James Beard's New Fish Cookery	202	207,050	3185.4
13	James Beard's Theory and Practice of Good Cooking	156	159,900	2460
14	Mastering the Art of French Cooking	242	248,050	3816.2
15	From Julia Child's Kitchen	227	232,675	3579.6
16	The Way to Cook	173.32	177,653	2733
17	The Best of British Cooking	71	72,775	1119.6
18	Mastering the Art of French Cooking, Volume II	170	174,250	2680.8
19	Manifold Destiny	13[57]	13,325	205
20	Beard on Bread	57	58,425	898.8
21	Pierre Franey's Low-Calorie Gourmet	61.2	62,730	965.1
22	Cuisine Minceur	12.32	12,628	194.3

continued from previous page
25 Unconvincing as an Italian.
26 Best line: "Here are grunions at their best."
27 Veggie/butter ratio drops to 6 tablespoons (see number 14).
28 JBI variation among four Julia books only 11.5 percent; good consistency.
29 Her first solo book.
30 A yuppie's first cookbook, emphasis on things to buy.
31 Shares publication date with *Manifold Destiny*, a very funny book.
32 Mashed potato recipe calls for only 2 tablespoons butter.
33 Square root of 2 multiplied by 4.
34 You must be kidding.
35 What happened to Louisette Bertholle?

Hours standing[48]	Hours dressing[49]	Hours chopping wood	Days sleeping	Days standing	Days chopping wood	Days dressing	Days in the life of an elephant[50]
1107	938.1	230.6	71	46.1	9.6	39.1	2.21
2391.5	2026.7	498.2[51]	153.3	99.6	20.8	84.4	4.78
2548.6	2159.8	531	163.4	106.2	22.1	90	5.1
1414.5	1198.7	294.7	90.7	58.9	12.3	49.9	2.83
4100	3474.6	854.2	262.8	170.8	35.6	144.8	8.2
5596.5	4742.8	1165.9	358.8	233.2	48.6	197.6	11.19
2712.6	2298.8	565.1	173.9	113	23.5	95.8	5.43
6154.1	5215.3	1282.1	394.5	256.4	53.4	217.3	12.31
1168.5	990.3	243.4	74.9	48.7	10.1[54]	41.3	2.34
1931.9	1637.2	402.5	123.8	80.5	16.8	68.2	3.86
742.9	629.6	154.8	47.6	31	6.5	26.2	1.49
2070.5	1754.7	431.4	132.7	86.3	18[56]	73.1	4.14
1599	1355.1	333.1	102.5	66.6	13.9	56.5	3.2
2480.5	2102.1	516.8	159	103.4	21.5	87.6	4.96
2326.8	1971.8	484.7	149.1	97	20.2	82.2	4.65
1776.6	1505.5	370.1	113.9	74	15.4	62.7	3.55
727.8	616.7	151.6	46.7	30.3	6.3	25.7	1.46
1742.5	1476.7	363	111.7	72.6	15.1	61.5	3.49
133.3	112.9	27.8	8.5	5.6	1.2	4.7	.27
584.3	495.1	121.7	37.5	24.3	5.1[58]	20.6	1.17
627.3	531.6	130.7	40.2	26.1	5.4	22.2	1.25
126.28	107	26.3	8.1	5.3	1.1	4.5	.25[59]

36 A very funny book, see number 39.
37 Yours truly.
38 Shares publication date with *The Way To Cook*, J. Child.
39 Weeks in year butter is in season in our state.
40 Another wonderful book.
41 Does not include suggested slatherings of butter on finished product.
42 Suggests big plates and thin slices to make diners think they've eaten more. Why not just serve more?
43 Third place, Even Cow award.
44 A stupid, overextended book.
45 Probably does not cast a shadow.
46 Might as well be teaspoons.

Rank	Title	Days in the life of a kangaroo	Same, chimpanzee	Same, silverback gorilla
1	The Buster Holmes Restaurant Cookbook	110.7	55.35	22.2
2	American Charcuterie	239.2	119.6	47.8
3	Chef Paul Prudhomme's Louisiana Kitchen	254.9	127.45	51
4	Foie Gras, Magret, and Other Good Food from Gascony	141.5	70.75	28.3
5	The New James Beard	410	205	82
6	The Fannie Farmer Cookbook	559.7	279.85	11.9
7	James Beard's Menus for Entertaining	271.3	135.65	54.3
8	James Beard's American Cookery	615.4	307.7	123.1
9	The Low Salt, Low Cholesterol Cookbook	116.9	58.45	23.4
10	The Fannie Farmer Cookbook	193.2	96.6	38.6
11	Beard on Pasta	74.3	37.15	14.9
12	James Beard's New Fish Cookery	207.1	103.55	41.4
13	James Beard's Theory and Practice of Good Cooking	159.9	79.95	32
14	Mastering the Art of French Cooking	248.1	124.05	49.6
15	From Julia Child's Kitchen	232.7	116.35	46.5
16	The Way to Cook	177.7	88.85	35.5
17	The Best of British Cooking	72.8	36.4	14.6
18	Mastering the Art of French Cooking, Volume II	174.3	87.15	34.9
19	Manifold Destiny	13.3	6.65	2.7
20	Beard on Bread	58.4	29.2	11.7
21	Pierre Franey's Low-Calorie Gourmet	62.7	31.35	12.5
22	Cuisine Minceur	12.6	6.3	2.5

continued from previous page

47 Twenty-four minutes of wasted energy if you're the least bit hungry.
48 Just standing around.
49 Dressing for dinner.
50 All animals shown are large adult males. *A day in the life* is one day of normal activity.
51 Boudin Noir recipe calls for "very fresh blood."
52 Again, we like the symmetry.
53 Ditto.
54 Ten days of chopping wood and you'll never go back on the diet.
55 Our parents' street number.
56 Draft registration age.
57 A pittance.

Same, tiger	Boxes of Cheerios	Mallomars	Chef Boyardee Beef Ravioli, 15 oz. cans[60]	Lean Cuisine Tuna Lasagna	Hellman's mayonnaise, quarts	Oreos
14.76	67.1	1845[61]	252	410	17.3	2,214
31.89	144.9	3986	544	886	37.37	4,783
33.98	154.5	4248	579	944	39.82	5,097
18.86	85.7	2358	321	524	22.1	2,829
54.67	248.5	6833	932	1519	64.06	8,200
74.62	339.2	9328	1272	2073	87.45	11,193
36.17	164.4	4521	616	1005	42.38	5,425
82.05	373	10,257	1399	2279	96.16	12,308
15.58	70.8	1948[62]	266	433	18.26	2,337
25.76	117.1	3220	439	716	30.19	3,864
9.91	45	1238	169	275	11.61	1,485
27.61	125.5	3451	471	767[63]	32.35	4,141
21.32	96.9	2665	363	592	24.98	3,198
33.07	150.3	4134	564	919	38.76	4,961
31.02	141	3878	529	862	36.36	4,654
23.69	107.7	2961	404	658	27.76	3,553
9.7	44.1	1213	165	270	11.37	1,456
23.23	105.6	2904	396	645	27.23	3,485
1.78	8.1	222	30	49	2.08	267
7.79	35.4	974	133	216	9.13	1,169
8.36	38	1046	143	232	9.8	1,255
1.68	7.7	210	28.7	47	1.97	253

58 Probably a lot more wood chopping than Fat Jim ever did himself.
59 No wonder elephants don't eat spa cuisine.
60 Much heartier than the cheese variety.
61 When in season.
62 The year one of us was born.
63 Boeing wide-body jet, serves food that tastes like Lean Cuisine.

Many thanks to the New York Zoological Society, and to Dr. James L. Shafland of the New York University School of Medicine.

CHAPTER 6

DESSERTS WORTHY OF THE NAME

WE HAVE BEEN puzzling, of late, over two contradictory trends in American eating habits. One is the shameful neglect of dessert, except in fern bars that offer mud pie and in chichi restaurants that swirl raspberry coulis into crème anglaise with a fork. And even in these places, you see more and more people just having the dessert, or having it after an appetizer, rather than enjoying it properly as the last course of a full meal and a palate-cleanser for walnuts and port. The other trend is the phenomenal rise of superpremium ice creams. All we can conclude is that, somehow, people don't think these are dessert, but rather a form of entertainment like movie rentals (the two often go together). We have another theory regarding the popularity of superpremium ice cream, and it has to do with the fact that when Ben and Jerry ran an 800 number on the sides of their containers, most of the people who called it did so at three in the morning. Hint: They were not just saying no.

But face it: Whether you're eating it because it's the hip thing to pass around to the people you invited over to watch *Dances with Wolves,* or because you have something in common with Bob Marley, *it's still dessert.* And that's very liberating to understand; once you know you're eating chocolate and sugar and cream anyway, you may as well investigate the rest of the dessert repertory—fruit dumplings, pie, éclairs, you name it. Then when the gang comes around to watch movies, you'll surprise them with big helpings of doughnut pudding. If they balk, repeat after us:

"I'll bet you'd eat doughnut-pudding ice cream if Ben and Jerry made it!"

• •

STEAM PONE

In the American South, pone is any breadlike substance based on cornmeal. Steam pone really expands the concept of "breadlike." Sure, it's got the usual stuff like meal and flour, fat, and something to make it rise. But after six hours of steaming and two of baking it resembles a drag anchor more than anything else. If this were made in New Jersey a lot of waterfront concrete block establishments would go down without even being chained to their product.

If this recipe is ever seen in the future, it will probably be accompanied by a Surgeon General's disclaimer: "Warning: This recipe provided only as an example of how far man can stray from the natural order."

> 2 cups whole wheat flour
> 5 cups white cornmeal
> 2 teaspoons baking soda
> 1 teaspoon salt
> 1 cup molasses
> 1 quart buttermilk

• Mix all ingredients well. Pour into mold or pot; cover very tightly. Place in large kettle filled with boiling water and steam for 6 hours. Unmold into baking dish and bake to dark brown, about 2 hours at 275°.

• •

DOUGHNUT PUDDING

Our first and never-repeated contact with doughnut pudding came in a small restaurant in Manchester, New Hampshire, during the 1980 presidential primaries. Situated near the middle of the city's main drag, it was the kind of place where we were the only ones there no one knew.

Doughnut pudding is actually pretty good since stale doughnuts give you something to chew as opposed to stale white bread. The pudding was different each day based on the previous day's doughnut consumption. Don't bother driving to Manchester to try it; the place has been panelled and now serves quiche, with a salad bar. That's why we're giving you the recipe.

Incidentally, they also served "Jell-O du jour." We asked what it was and the waitress answered, "Red."

> 6 stale cake doughnuts or crullers (Do not use jelly
> doughnuts)
> 1 cup raisins
> 4 eggs
> 1½ cups milk
> 1 cup heavy cream
> 3 tablespoons sugar

- Chop or break doughnuts into small pieces. Mix with raisins. Beat the eggs until frothy, then beat in milk, cream, and sugar. Stir until sugar is dissolved.
- Grease a baking dish and add the doughnut/raisin mixture. Pour egg mixture over all and let stand for 15 minutes.
- Set dish in roasting pan containing enough boiling water to come halfway up side of pudding dish. Place in 375° oven until center is set, about 20 minutes.

● ●

These desserts are from the repertory of the Pennsylvania Dutch, who have a saying that goes, "Better a burst stomach than wasted food." Right to the point, those people. They also have a cheerier, less drastic bit of doggerel, "Shoofly pie and apple pandowdy/Make your eyes light up and your stomach say howdy."

We don't know what the etymology of these two dishes is. Apple pandowdy just sounds satisfying; as to the other one, we suspect entomology might be more like it. Could it be that in the days before screen doors, the molasses content of the pie in question was enough to keep flies off everything else on the table? And although it has nothing to do with flies, we ought to pass along something else we read about shoofly. When the Pennsylvania Dutch set one of their typical burst-before-you-waste tables, they put a pie out at the beginning so dessert-firsters don't have to be embarrassed to ask for it.

APPLE PANDOWDY

  1 loaf Boston brown bread (available in cans in certain parts
      of country)
     butter at room temperature
2½ pounds tart apples
  5 tablespoons brown sugar, firmly packed
     cinnamon
  2 cups whipped cream with ¼ cup sugar beaten in

- Slice brown bread thinly and butter well. Line a greased baking dish with half the slices. Peel, core, and slice the apples, and spread in a layer over the bread. Sprinkle with the sugar and cinnamon to taste. Pour over all ½ cup hot water. Cover with remaining bread, placed butter-side up. Bake 1 hour at 300°. Serve with whipped cream on side.

● ●

SHOOFLY PIE

    1 cup molasses
    1 cup boiling water
    2 eggs
    ½ teaspoon salt
  1½ teaspoons baking soda
    4 cups flour
    ½ cup lard, chilled
  1½ cups sugar
    1 10-inch piecrust, uncooked
       cinnamon
       nutmeg

- Add molasses to boiling water in mixing bowl; stir to dissolve. Beat eggs and add to bowl along with salt and ½ teaspoon of the baking soda.
- In another bowl mix flour, lard, sugar, and remaining teaspoon baking soda. Using fingertips, work mixture until it resembles bread crumbs.
- Pour molasses/egg mixture into pie shell. Spread flour/lard crumbs evenly over top. Sprinkle with cinnamon and nutmeg. Bake 10 minutes at 425°, then about 25 minutes at 350°.

FRUIT DUMPLINGS WITH CRÈME ANGLAISE

Crème anglaise is the result of experiments designed to modify custard so that it could be taken intravenously. It's also one of the few dishes that proudly advertises its English origins, albeit in French. Crème anglaise is not only a perfect foil for fruit dumplings, but a worthwhile alternative to hard sauce as a topping for Plum Pudding (page 130). As for the fruit dumplings, traditional and modern schools differ greatly regarding the application of the sauce. The traditional way is to plop a dumpling on a plate, and then pour sauce over it. The new technique is to pour sauce in the bottom of the plate, and put the dumpling on top. This looks nice, but we associate it with the kind of restaurants that serve you a puddle of sauce three microns thick, with designs swirled into it by a guy with a fork dipped in a pink coulis, accompanied by a two-inch-square slice of chocolate pâte, a mint leaf, and a single raspberry ($8.25). Our solution? The perfect compromise: two layers of crème anglaise, with a fruit dumpling in the middle.

Fruit Dumplings

- 2 cups flour
- ½ teaspoon salt
- 2¾ teaspoons baking powder
- 4 tablespoons sugar
- 5 tablespoons butter, chilled
- ⅔ cup milk, approximately
- 2 cups fruit (cherries, fresh apricots, peach halves, pear halves, etc.)
- 2 tablespoons brown sugar, firmly packed
- 4 tablespoons water

Crème Anglaise
     1 whole egg plus 5 yolks
     ¼ cup sugar
        dash of salt
     2 cups milk
     1 tablespoon cognac

- To prepare dumplings, sift together flour, salt, baking powder, and 1 tablespoon of the white sugar. Add butter and work with fingertips until well mixed. Add milk in small amounts until dough forms. Knead lightly about 1 minute, until smooth.

- Roll dough, using floured rolling pin on well-floured surface, to ¼-inch thickness. Cut into 6 squares. In center of each square place ⅓ cup fruit and sprinkle with ½ tablespoon white sugar. Wrap dough around fruit in neat package; brush edges with milk or water to form good seal.

- Dissolve brown sugar in water; cover bottom of greased baking dish with the syrup. Add dumplings, seam-side down. Bake about 40 minutes at 375°, basting with syrup.

- Meanwhile, make the crème anglaise by lightly beating together egg and yolks. Mix in sugar and salt. Bring milk to boil and pour into egg mixture. Place in clean saucepan and cook over extremely low heat, stirring constantly, until mixture coats the spoon. Stir in cognac. Spoon crème anglaise onto plate *and* over dumpling.

●   ●

TRIFLE

There are two reasons why people don't make trifle. The first is that it sounds frivolous to the point of being apocryphal, as in "What is trifle, anyway?" To these people, trifle is in a category with the fantods, or runcible spoons—too fey and Victorian to be real. The other reason prevails among people who have actually had trifle, probably in England, and think that it's supposed to be a sickly sweet mass of congealed glop. But trifle is real enough, and, no, it's not categorically awful.

  1 whole egg plus 5 yolks
 ¼ cup sugar
    dash of salt
  2 cups milk
 ½ teaspoon vanilla
    stale sponge cake
    jam (raspberry, strawberry, or apricot are best)
  4 ounces good sherry
    whipped cream

- Beat egg and yolks lightly, then mix in sugar and salt. Bring milk to boil and pour into egg mixture. Place in clean saucepan and cook over extremely low heat, stirring constantly, until mixture coats the spoon. Add vanilla and pour into bowl.
- Split sponge cake horizontally and arrange half to cover bottom of serving dish. Spread with jam, cover with remaining cake. Sprinkle sherry over cake and let sit for a half hour. Pour custard over all and place in refrigerator to set. To serve, top with whipped cream and a few dollops of the jam.

RICE PUDDING

A custard, nothing more or less, fortified with rice. The rice puddings of our youth were usually made from a Minute box, and they weren't bad, but here we offer the traditional version. For some reason this is everyone's all-time favorite "comfort food," although our personal vote would be for potato croquettes (page 88).

    ½ cup raw rice
    2 quarts milk
    ½ cup raisins, chopped
    3 tablespoons sugar
       dash of nutmeg

- Mix all ingredients and pour into pudding dish. Place in 325° oven for 2 hours. After 15 minutes, stir well, taking care to push crust down into pudding. Repeat at 30-minute, 45-minute, 1-hour, and 1½-hour marks.

LARD CAKE

At first the name threw us for a loop, but we managed to warm to it. We have, after all, traveled several hours out of our way just so we could say we've been to a small town below Stockton, California, named Manteca (which just happens to be Spanish for lard).

Lard cake is where Southern tradition, poverty, and the American chemical industry intersect. During that long stretch between the Civil War and World War II, many people in the South lived on close to nothing. One endearing custom that evolved was the "community sinker," a chunk of fatback or a ham bone, which, string attached, made the rounds of everyone's pot of beans or greens. Even when no one had the money to buy real meat, food still had enough fat molecules clinging to it to make people feel fed.

This "fed" feeling turns out to be as much in the mouth as in the stomach. When some of our larger food giants (which are really chemical refineries) got onto the idea of artificial fat, they discovered that the taste of fat exists to a large extent in the feel of fat. What they have wound up with are microscopic round granules that mimic the ball-bearing effect of real fat. It's about the same gulf as exists between a crazed Earl Long giving a stem-winder and the apparition of a Ronald Reagan reading a TelePrompTer.

Poverty steps to the plate in the form of lard, both cheap and plentiful.

     2 eggs
  1½ cups sugar
     ½ cup lard, softened
  2½ cups flour, sifted
     1 teaspoon salt
     1 tablespoon baking powder
     ¾ cup evaporated milk mixed with ⅓ cup water
  1½ teaspoons vanilla

- Separate eggs; beat whites until frothy. Beat in ½ cup of the sugar; keep beating until whites form stiff peaks.
- In another mixing bowl cream lard with remaining cup of sugar. When softened add flour, salt, and baking powder. Beat for about a minute. Add egg yolks, evaporated milk mixed with water, and vanilla and mix well.
- Carefully fold in egg white mixture. Bake in 3-by-4-by-12-inch buttered cake tin for 30 minutes in a 350° oven.

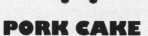

PORK CAKE

Anything said about lard cake holds true for pork cake, except that salt pork in Spanish is tocino, *and there's no town in California named for it.*

½   pound fatty salt pork, finely ground
1¼ cups boiling water
 5 cups flour
1¼ teaspoons baking soda
½   teaspoon salt
2½ teaspoons baking powder
 1 teaspoon each nutmeg, ground cloves, and cinnamon
 2 eggs
½   cup sugar
1½ cups molasses
 1 cup minced currants

- Put ground salt pork in heat-proof bowl and add boiling water. Set aside for a half hour, stirring occasionally.
- Sift together all dry ingredients except sugar.
- Pour pork and water into large mixing bowl. Beat in eggs, followed by sugar and molasses. Add dry ingredients and currants and stir to mix well.
- Grease and flour 2 9-by-4-inch bread pans. Divide batter between them and bake at 325° for 1 hour. Cakes are done when they have the resiliency of a medium-rare steak.

CHOCOLATE SNAP- WHIPPED CREAM CAKE

This is a recipe we saw once on a bag of chocolate snaps. It looked stupid enough to work, and it did.

20 to 25 chocolate snap cookies
½ pint heavy cream, whipped with 1 teaspoon sugar

- On a long serving platter, arrange chocolate snaps in a log shape about ⅜ inch apart, using whipped cream as mortar between each snap. Save enough whipped cream to frost the log and ends. Cover the platter with plastic wrap, and put the "cake" into the refrigerator for 4 to 6 hours. The whipped cream will soak into the chocolate snaps, causing them to expand and get soft (this is what happened to us). By dessert time, you'll be able to slice off diagonal slabs, and your guests will think you slaved all day making devil's food.

• •

SPLENDID DATE-CUSTARD PIE

Back in the fifties there was a restaurant called the Splendid in Portland, Maine, where this unusual pie was a specialty. We have never seen it anywhere else, which may be due to the fact that no one but the Splendid's pastry chef could figure out how to get the chopped dates to stay evenly distributed in the custard and not sink to the bottom. We've tried throwing them in the blender with the custard mixture, chopping them so fine that the individual particles are lighter than custard molecules, and even mixing them in partway through baking, when the custard is already partly set (a messy procedure, and not recommended). Finally we figured what the hell, it tastes good even if the dates are on the bottom, and gave up. Let us know if you come up with any solutions.

    4 eggs
   ⅔ cup sugar
   ½ teaspoon salt
  2⅔ cups milk
    I teaspoon vanilla
    I cup finely chopped pitted dates
    9 - inch unbaked piecrust

• Preheat oven to 425°. Beat eggs with a rotary beater, then add sugar, salt, milk, and vanilla. Add dates. Pour mixture into piecrust. Bake 15 minutes, then reduce oven temperature to 350°. Bake about 30 minutes longer, or until a knife inserted into custard 1 inch from edge of pie comes out clean.

● ●

TRANCHETTE

This easy dessert recipe comes to us from the ultimate cold-climate (read "heavy") cuisine, that of French Canada. This is our own adaptation of a dish we always order at Les Filles du Roi, a restaurant in Montreal, when the caribou tortiere and roast suckling pig have failed to fill us up. Ideally, you should follow such a meal by clearing a few hundred acres of the St. Lawrence Valley and fighting the French and Indian War, but good sense usually prevails and we saunter up to the Ritz for a cognac instead.

> 4 tablespoons butter
> 4 thick slices of good-quality white bread, crust removed
> I pint heavy cream
> ½ cup 100 percent pure Quebec or Vermont maple syrup

- In a heavy frying pan, heat butter until bubbling and fry bread until lightly browned on both sides, being careful not to burn butter. Remove bread slices and put one slice in each of 4 dessert cups (balloon wine glasses are an elegant option). Heat the heavy cream and maple syrup in separate saucepans until warm (not hot). Pour the syrup evenly around the bread slices in the bottom of each cup or glass, and top off evenly with the cream, pouring carefully so a minimum amount of mixing of syrup and cream takes place. Serve immediately.

● ●

BLACKWATCH HOT FUDGE SAUCE

This dense and tasty dessert topping is not connected with the famous British regiment of the same name. It just so happens that we were given the recipe at a place called Blackwatch Well in Bermuda, so named because members of the regiment once dug a well there. The first time we made it, we brought it a little too far past the soft-ball stage, and wished that a few regimental stalwarts had been there with their pickaxes to quarry through the impervious glassy mass to reach the ice cream below. In any event, this stuff constitutes the ultimate challenge to Poli-grip.

  1 cup sugar
  4 tablespoons unsweetened cocoa powder
  ½ cup heavy cream
  1 teaspoon vanilla
  2 tablespoons butter

• In a heavy saucepan, mix sugar and cocoa and stir over medium heat with a wooden spoon until sugar melts to a smooth liquid. This will take a few minutes, so be patient. Add heavy cream, and stir to mix completely. Let simmer gently until slightly past the soft-ball stage. (If you're not a candy maker, ''soft ball'' means the point at which a drop of the sugar mixture, allowed to fall into a glass of cold water, will form a soft ball. Have your cold water handy, and *keep testing*. The next stage is called ''hard ball,'' meaning just what you think. This is where we got into trouble.) Remove from heat, add vanilla and butter, and stir. The sauce is now ready to pour over ice cream, preferably atop a brownie.

● ●

CREAM PUFFS/ÉCLAIRS

Cream puffs and éclairs have provided a few significant moments in our lives. (A few ungenerous sorts have suggested perhaps too many moments of too much significance.)

Most people have heard the old story of the city kid who goes to the country for the first time and doesn't realize that a cow is the original container for milk, and probably spends the next five years thinking that white milk comes from white cows and chocolate from Brown Swiss. For us, the éclair is the first food we realized had actually been constructed. *Although we'd naturally seen Mom make sandwiches, and we'd helped Gram peel the apples for pie, it somehow had never occurred to us that God's grand design included rules for making éclairs.*

Two bites into a supermarket-bakery éclair, we looked at the neat cross section and saw the hands removing the crust from the oven, stuffing it with a large wad of creamy custard, then slathering on the chocolate topping. It was like reading a Golden Book on how to build a skyscraper or a nuclear submarine. Things got made. *People* made *them. It was possible to* make *something without a hammer and nails.*

The cream puff epiphany came along a lot later. To celebrate one of our thirtieth birthdays, the other of us made the world's largest (or at least West Newbury, Massachusetts's largest) cream puff. We just doubled the recipe for a normal batch of puffs, and baked the thing in a four-quart Pyrex casserole. A vat of custard later, the behometh was ready for fun. Unfortunately, this was before the days of home video cameras, so no record exists of the birthday boy's beaming, cherubic face as he ate nearly the whole thing.

Pastry

  ½ cup butter
  ¼ teaspoon salt
  I cup water
  I cup flour, sifted
  4 eggs

Filling

  ½ cup flour
  ½ teaspoon salt
  ⅔ cup sugar
  2 cups milk, at boiling point
  2 eggs, beaten
  I teaspoon vanilla

- To make pastry, bring butter, salt, and water to a boil together. Dump flour in and stir quickly over medium-high heat, until mixture forms a mass and pulls away from sides of pan. Let cool a bit, then add eggs, one at a time, beating well after each addition.
- Butter a baking sheet and put heaping tablespoons of dough down for cream puffs, or long mounds for éclairs, spacing well to allow for expansion. Bake at 450° for 15 minutes, reduce heat to 325°, and continue baking for another 25 minutes. Lift off with spatula and let cool on rack.
- To make filling, mix dry ingredients, then slowly mix in milk. Transfer to double boiler; add the eggs, and cook slowly for 2 minutes. Add vanilla and cool.
- To fill, put cooled filling into pastry bag with long spout. Cut tops off cream puffs, or hole in one end of éclairs, and scoop out any uncooked dough. Fill with appropriate amount of filling.
- Variations: For chocolate filling, let 2 ounces unsweetened chocolate melt as milk rises to the boil. For coffee filling, add 5 tablespoons ground coffee to milk as it nears boiling point. Stir and let boil 2 minutes. Strain before adding to filling.

● ●

PLUM PUDDING

Here's the ultimate yuletide pièce de résistance, a dish that will add an unmistakable Dickensian air to your holiday celebration and brighten your refrigerator for months to come. Months? At various junctures, we've had several vintages of plum pudding in the fridge at the same time, so that when we are queried as to whether it ought to be thrown out, we have to ask, "Which year are you talking about?" The truth is, plum pudding never has to be thrown out. You could stock a fallout shelter with the stuff and emerge hale and fit halfway through the twenty-first century. During the course of its nurturing, in the month between Thanksgiving and Christmas, it absorbs more rum than your humble correspondents on a hot night in Jamaica, and it cannot go bad under any circumstances short of being injected with penicillin and left in the sun.

We like to serve it on Christmas night, after everybody's had a couple of hours to digest their dinner. Unmold it (the mixing bowl from a KitchenAid K5SS, with muslin tied around the top, works great as a pudding mold) about half an hour after the boiling's done, and turn it out onto a platter that you'll decorate with holly sprigs. Turn off the lights, douse the pudding with a quarter cup of warm cognac, light it on fire, and bear it proudly into your great hall. Have the hard sauce ready, and serve small slices to the uninitiated and faint of heart. It's a heady concoction.

1½ cups currants
 2 cups raisins
 ¾ cup prunes
 2 cups candied fruit (orange peel, lemon peel, etc.)
 1 pound beef suet, well cleaned
    juice and grated zest of 1 lemon
    juice and grated zest of 1 orange
 5 cups homemade bread crumbs
2½ cups flour
 1 cup chopped almonds
 2 cups peeled and chopped cooking apples
1½ cups brown sugar, firmly packed
 1 tablespoon each ginger, cinnamon, and grated nutmeg
 2 teaspoons salt
 1 quart rum or cognac
 4 eggs

- Wash currants, raisins, and prunes. Chop prunes. Mince candied fruit. Mince the suet.
- Add all ingredients except rum or cognac and eggs to large bowl. Stir to mix very well. Add 1 cup of the liquor and stir again. Cover bowl with clean towel and put in cool place.
- Uncover every day, add 2 tablespoons rum or cognac and stir well. Recover. Continue until all but ¼ cup of the liquor is added. Pudding can stand 2 to 4 weeks.
- When ready to cook, add the eggs. Mixture may be thinned a bit with milk if necessary. Butter and flour mold. Add pudding mixture and cover with clean cotton cloth, tying securely with string. Set mold in large pot of boiling water and boil at least 6 hours.
- Remove and let stand 30 minutes. Unmold onto serving platter, anoint with the remaining cognac and ignite as instructed above, and serve hard sauce (see below).

•

HARD SAUCE FOR PLUM PUDDING

  1 cup sweet butter, softened
  2 cups confectioners' sugar
1½ teaspoons vanilla
  3 tablespoons brandy
    freshly grated nutmeg

• Thoroughly cream butter. Beat sugar in gradually, as if making mayonnaise. Add vanilla and brandy, beating gradually. Pour into serving bowl and grate nutmeg lightly over surface. Chill until needed.

ON STARTING
YOUR OWN
CLEAN PLATE CLUB

•

O KAY, ENOUGH ABOUT us. Let's talk about you. What do
you think about us? Over the years we've spent researching and writing this book, we've caught a lot of flak for our lines
of inquiry. After a while friends would try to change the subject
when we started jabbering about a week spent in Louisiana
eating everything fried except the salads and coffee. We'd go into
supermarkets to admire a particularly well-stocked lard display
and shoppers would turn away. Neighboring passengers on
airplanes would ask to change their seat assignments.

Just as we don't like to eat alone in restaurants, we don't
like to think we're the only ones who enjoy some nice fat
molecules careening off our taste buds. Looking for strength in
numbers, we wrote to a number of fellow chefs and cookbook
writers asking the Big Question: If you were to make a dish that
would blow all dietary caution to the winds, what would it be?

Surprise, surprise: a number of them never replied. Maybe
we should have enclosed stamped envelopes, but surely folks
like Craig Claiborne, Pierre Franey, and Julia Child could have
sprung for the 29 cents. Ditto for a few other of America's
cooking stars.

Still, replies did trickle in. The manager of Spago, the West
Hollywood spot where one eats little and is seen a lot, wrote
with apologies from Wolfgang Puck, owner, chef, and star. Mr.
Puck was "under severe pressure to finish his own book—long
overdue . . ."; he was "unable to offer (us) any assistance with
recipes for (our) book." We wondered about this. Here's a

restaurant that specializes in small portions of undercooked food at high prices; to a normal observer, he'd have all the time in the world on his hands. Surely, it can't take much more time to write about food like that than it does to cook it. What's he doing, spelling the book out in carrot sticks? Still, we were gratified to see that they "look forward to seeing it in the bookstore," which to us is not the same as buying it.

We tried Northern California, but Alice Waters, of Berkeley's Chez Panisse, said, "Nothing unfortunately comes to mind." Bear in mind that one of her cookbooks, on pasta, pizza, and calzone, cautions, "Avoid too much cheese!"; we feel it indeed unfortunate, especially for her. Of course, at the time of her letter she was "deep into salads and olive oil"; that's happened to us a few times but we always managed to escape.

Finally, serious eaters started to reply (maybe they needed time to finish dinner). Jane Brody, the "Personal Health" columnist for *The New York Times*, came up with an entry worthy of inclusion in our chapter "Ethnic Heavyweights." Noting that she would be "totally ignoring what I know to be the precepts of a wholesome diet" she offered a briefing on blinis with caviar: "Blinis—made with sweet butter (nearly pure fat) topped with melted butter (more fat and cholesterol), Beluga caviar (almost *pure* cholesterol—it *is* fish eggs, after all), real (not light) sour cream (more fat and cholesterol), chopped hard-boiled eggs (more of the same), and minced red onion (the only health-promoting ingredient—sorry, but onion DOES enhance this dish)." We don't mind the red onion at all, being fans of enhancement. Ms. Brody closes by noting, "With champagne, it is the best New Year's Eve supper I can imagine." As far as we're concerned it makes a damn fine light breakfast, too. Since getting her letter, we've faithfully read her weekly column. Thanks.

● ●

A FEW DAYS LATER we heard from what we thought an unlikely source. Carolyn Kelly, assistant to Martha Stewart, called to see if we still needed recipes. "Sure," we said, and soon received a well-stuffed envelope. We were delighted to hear from Ms. Stewart, who not only writes cookbooks but offers seminars on collecting and living well, does television shows, and is one of the few people around who has a magazine named after her. We really thought she'd be too busy out decorating the world to help a couple of butterfat munchkins like us. (Hear that, Wolfgang?) Of Ms. Stewart's two recipes, we're passing along her "paskha," mainly because the yield is described as "1 very large paskha." We'd never heard of paskha before, but that phrase "very large" must have struck a chord. The recipe doesn't indicate servings, so we figure two or three, maybe.

•

PASKHA

Paskha is a crowning glory of the Easter table, the rich cheesecake that symbolizes the end of Lent and its prohibition of dairy products. The traditional paskha mold can be replaced by a tapered clay flowerpot eight inches in diameter, and the decorations (ours are dried fruits) can be as fantastic as you want.

    2 pounds fresh farmer cheese
    6 egg yolks
 1 ½ cups sugar
    1 cup heavy cream
    ¾ pound (3 sticks) unsalted butter at room temperature
    ¼ teaspoon grated nutmeg
      zest of 1 orange
    ⅓ cup candied citron or lemon peel, finely chopped
    2 tablespoons vanilla extract (optional)
      assorted dried fruits for decoration

- With the back of a wooden spoon, press the farmer cheese through a medium strainer. In a mixer, beat together the egg yolks and sugar at high speed until a ribbon forms, about 5 minutes. Reduce speed; add the cheese, heavy cream, butter, nutmeg, orange zest, and candied fruit, and combine until very smooth. Add vanilla and/or additional sugar to taste if desired.

- Line the paskha mold or flowerpot with dampened cheesecloth, and add batter; fold excess cheesecloth over the top. Put a plate or flat cake round on top of the cheesecloth, and weight it down (about 5 pounds is good) to compress the batter. Put the filled mold over an empty pot; let drain overnight in the refrigerator.

- Remove the weight and plate or cake round. Carefully invert the mold onto a plate and lift it off; remove cheesecloth. Decorate with additional dried fruits and serve.

WHO SAYS GREAT minds don't think alike? First read our Bread Soufflé recipe, page 113, from the wilds of northern Rhode Island. Now consider Jane and Michael Stern, authors of *Square Meals* and *Good Food*, who seem to have spent a good part of their lives following some of the same trails we've slogged along. (The Sterns once did a piece in *The New Yorker* on nudists; we once spent a journalistic week in the company of two of their larger interviewees. Jane and Michael were delighted to hear we had christened this expansive couple "The Potatoes." Food is a constant in many lives.) They live in the wilds of Connecticut, about 120 miles from the source of the bread soufflé, and, what do they come up with? White bread pinwheels, lined with cheese and condensed mushroom soup, surrounded by fatty bacon. We'd be the first (or first two) to admit they have the edge in technological sophistication and presentation, but they're part of the New York metropolitan area, and one of us is just a swamp Yankee. Their "Raparees" are great enough to put a kink in any purist's diet. It takes a lot of nerve to take *white* bread, overprocessed and ripe with chemicals (see "From Whence They Came," page 61) add some factory-produced imitation soup and a dash of cow's cholesterol, and then surround it with a lashing of the ultimate evil, the hog. They even have the lack of couth to leave out fancy herbs.

The only thing we can't figure out is the name of the dish. Maybe it's something out of the mouth of a nitrate-crazed pig eater, trying to say "wrap-arounds" but giving up after the second syllable? The Sterns blame this one on a friend of theirs, Ben Van Vechten. Sorry Ben, they brought it up.

•

RAPAREES

8 slices Arnold white bread
½ can Golden Mushroom Soup
4 ounces grated Swiss cheese
12 strips cheap, thin bacon

- Remove crust from bread; cut each slice into thirds. Using a pastry brush, spread each piece generously with soup. Sprinkle with cheese.
- Lay each piece of bread on ½ slice of room temperature, uncooked bacon, roll like a jelly roll, and set on baking sheet, seam-down. Use a toothpick if necessary to keep raparees firmly together. They may be chilled until baked. Bake at 300° 30–40 minutes or until well browned.

OUR FINAL GRACIOUS contributor to this cascade of gluttony is the well-known writer and television star/cook, Jeff Smith. Jeff lives in Seattle, which, besides being a veritable, if somewhat damp, paradise of the Northwest, is also the home of the Pike Street Market. For those who have never been there, the Pike Street Market is the closest we've ever come to the markets of France, where every display makes us wish we had a good kitchen nearby, so we could fill our arms with raw materials, run home, and make something! Imagine tray after tray of the finest produce, all artfully arranged, interspersed with glistening seafood and butcher shops full of the cuts of meat that embarrass shy shoppers who never thought that their food was at one time raw, which is only one step removed from living. It's also the only place we've ever seen geoducks, cocker-spaniel-size clams, which cry out to be steamed and served sliced like a London broil.

Again, we digress, but Jeff's a chatty guy and so are we. He seemed quite delighted with our effort to show that long life and gustatory bliss can exist side-by-side; indeed, his show usually exudes delight in how good food is and how much fun it is to cook, because then you get to sit down with others and eat!

His "Cassoulet Corpulent" brought even us to a momentary standstill, until we realized, that despite its similarity to our Cholent recipe, page 114, his doesn't have any potatoes. But who's counting, after you get past the goose, the ribs, the beans, the lamb breast, the *pork jowl*, plus the final Polish sausage? He claims he's had it, at times when he "need(s) to leave the table knowing that I have eaten, really eaten. This is my favorite food when I need such support and fulfillment." Our guest chef points out that it's not really as complicated as it seems; just "read it through a couple of times before beginning and you will be quite comfortable . . . and eventually quite corpulent." We don't own any stock in tall and large men's stores, but it's spirit like this that tempts us to call our brokers.

•

CASSOULET CORPULENT

1 cleaned goose or duck (I prefer goose) defrosted if frozen and cut into serving pieces
2 pounds pork spareribs, cut into single ribs
2 pounds small white beans, soaked overnight
  chicken soup stock or fresh water
2 whole yellow onions, peeled and stuck with 2 cloves
4 carrots, quartered
3 cloves garlic, peeled and crushed
1 1-pound piece lamb breast
1½ pounds smoked pork jowl, skin removed, or salt pork, rinsed
2 tablespoons butter
2 tablespoons peanut oil
3 cups finely chopped yellow onions
1 teaspoon crushed garlic
1 cup tomato puree
  salt and freshly ground black pepper to taste
1 Polish sausage, cut up

- Brown the poultry pieces in the oven along with the pork spareribs at 350° until barely browned, about ½ hour.
- Drain the beans and place in a large kettle with a metal lid that can be placed in the oven, or use a very large casserole. Cover the beans with chicken soup stock or water and add the yellow onions, stuck with cloves, the carrots, and the 3 cloves of garlic. Tie the lamb breast and smoked pork jowl or salt pork into a little bundle (simply use string and tie it up!). Place the bundle in the pot with the beans and vegetables. Cook gently, covered, for about 1 hour, or until the beans are about half-cooked.
- In the meantime, in a frying pan, melt a little butter. Add a little peanut oil and sauté the finely chopped onions and the 1 teaspoon garlic for about 4 minutes. Add the tomato puree and a little salt and pepper to the pan. Set aside.
- When the beans are half-done, remove the lamb and smoked jowl and cut them into bite-size pieces. Add to the frying pan mixture. Mix and cook for a few minutes.
- To the pot of beans and vegetables add the cut-up cooked poultry and spareribs, and the cut-up Polish sausage. Simmer for another 30 minutes.
- Now we are ready!
- Remove everything from the big pot if you are going to bake in it, or get a large casserole. Place a layer of the beans and vegetables in the bottom of the casserole, add a layer of the tomato sauce, and top with another layer of beans. Continue this until all ingredients are in the casserole. Cover the top with a piece of buttered wax paper, and place the lid on the casserole. Bake in a 350° oven for about 1½ hours, adding a little stock or water if needed to prevent it from drying out.
- Serve on large plates with a green salad on the side.

● ●

KAY, CRY "UNCLE"? Had enough? We haven't; we've been perusing this whole section as an hors d'oeuvre section on a rather extended menu. Jeff Smith described his cassoulet as containing a "burden . . . of guilt." We're not putting words into his mouth (the cassoulet seems quite enough) but we think he might have slipped past "burden of glut."

After a decade or so of disgustingly conspicuous consumption, a lot of people seem to want to pretend it all never happened, that we never spawned a populace intent on having every meal delivered to them, whether by waiter or messenger, anything to avoid having anything to do with it except paying a hefty price (for conversational points) to said waiter or messenger. As we move into whatever phase of the post-industrial revolution, what's been forgotten is that you feed people because you love them. You want to see your family and friends satisfied and well fed, not just caught up on arugula or cilantro or whatever the hell it is this week. We didn't get this far by not eating.

It's okay to eat large portions. It's okay to eat the food your mother fed you, especially if she learned it from her mother. It's okay to order mashed potatoes in a fancy restaurant, unless they charge you $8.95, in which case you've been rooked. You won't be shipped over to Hell if you make a meat loaf with bread filling; you won't go into cardiac arrest if you chow down on a steak.

It's okay. Calm down.

THE NORTHEAST

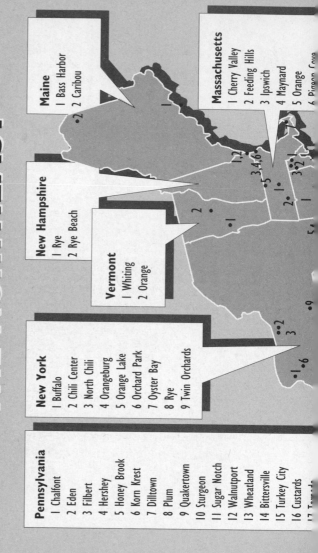

Maine
1 Bass Harbor
2 Caribou

New Hampshire
1 Rye
2 Rye Beach

Vermont
1 Whiting
2 Orange

Massachusetts
1 Cherry Valley
2 Feeding Hills
3 Ipswich
4 Maynard
5 Orange
6 Pigeon Cove

New York
1 Buffalo
2 Chili Center
3 North Chili
4 Orangeburg
5 Orange Lake
6 Orchard Park
7 Oyster Bay
8 Rye
9 Twin Orchards

Pennsylvania
1 Chalfont
2 Eden
3 Filbert
4 Hershey
5 Honey Brook
6 Korn Krest
7 Dilltown
8 Plum
9 Quakertown
10 Sturgeon
11 Sugar Notch
12 Walnutport
13 Wheatland
14 Bittersville
15 Turkey City
16 Custards

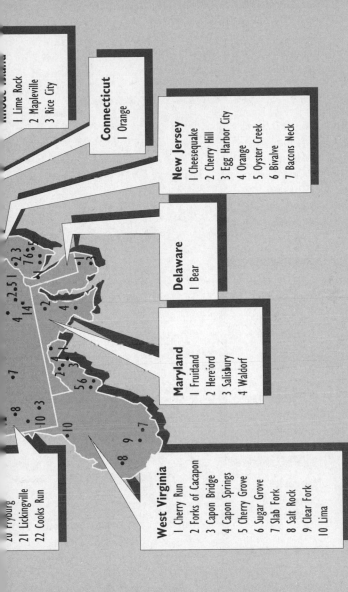

Connecticut
1 Orange

1 Lime Rock
2 Mapleville
3 Rice City

New Jersey
1 Cheesequake
2 Cherry Hill
3 Egg Harbor City
4 Orange
5 Oyster Creek
6 Bivalve
7 Bacons Neck

Delaware
1 Bear

Maryland
1 Fruitland
2 Here'ord
3 Salisbury
4 Waldorf

West Virginia
1 Cherry Run
2 Forks of Cacapon
3 Capon Bridge
4 Capon Springs
5 Cherry Grove
6 Sugar Grove
7 Slab Fork
8 Salt Rock
9 Clear Fork
10 Lima

20 Fryburg
21 Lickingville
22 Cooks Run

TH

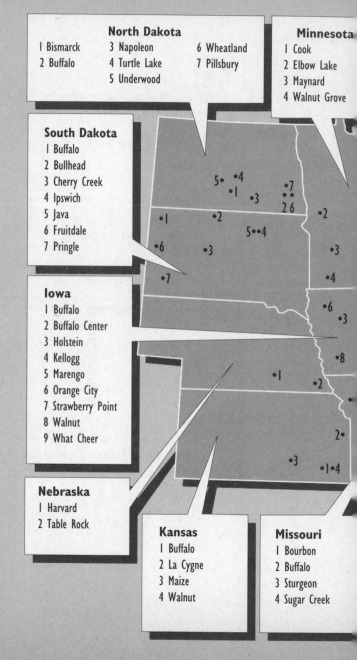

North Dakota

1 Bismarck   3 Napoleon   6 Wheatland
2 Buffalo   4 Turtle Lake   7 Pillsbury
   5 Underwood

Minnesota

1 Cook
2 Elbow Lake
3 Maynard
4 Walnut Grove

South Dakota

1 Buffalo
2 Bullhead
3 Cherry Creek
4 Ipswich
5 Java
6 Fruitdale
7 Pringle

Iowa

1 Buffalo
2 Buffalo Center
3 Holstein
4 Kellogg
5 Marengo
6 Orange City
7 Strawberry Point
8 Walnut
9 What Cheer

Nebraska

1 Harvard
2 Table Rock

Kansas

1 Buffalo
2 La Cygne
3 Maize
4 Walnut

Missouri

1 Bourbon
2 Buffalo
3 Sturgeon
4 Sugar Creek

MIDWEST

Wisconsin

1 Buffalo
2 Egg Harbor
3 Land O'Lakes
4 Rib Lake
5 Rice Lake
6 Sturgeon Bay
7 Turtle Lake
8 Whitefish Bay
9 Whiting
10 Fish Creek
11 White Fish Bay
12 Dairyland
13 Almond
14 Chili

Michigan

1 Coldwater
2 Colon
3 Napoleon
4 Pigeon
5 White Pigeon

Ohio

1 Apple Creek
2 Buffalo
3 Farmersville
4 Fruit Hill
5 Frytown
6 Madeira
7 Parma
8 Pepper Pike
9 Salineville

Indiana

1 Bass Lake
2 Bourbon
3 Fish Lake
4 Knox
5 Marengo
6 Spiceland

Illinois

1 Bismarck
2 Buffalo Grove
3 Fruitland
4 Walnut

THE WEST

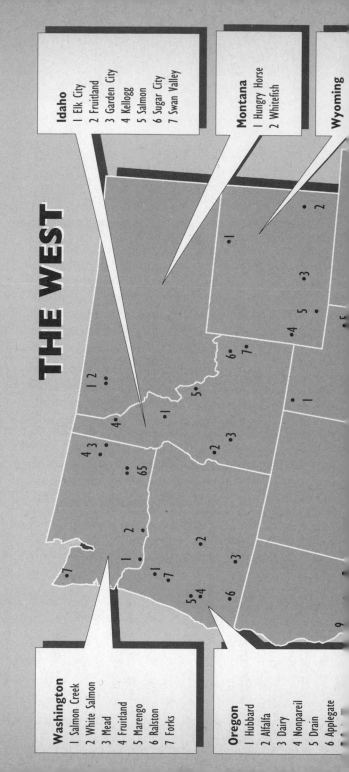

Idaho
1 Elk City
2 Fruitland
3 Garden City
4 Kellogg
5 Salmon
6 Sugar City
7 Swan Valley

Montana
1 Hungry Horse
2 Whitefish

Wyoming

Washington
1 Salmon Creek
2 White Salmon
3 Mead
4 Fruitland
5 Marengo
6 Ralston
7 Forks

Oregon
1 Hubbard
2 Alfalfa
3 Dairy
4 Nonpareil
5 Drain
6 Applegate

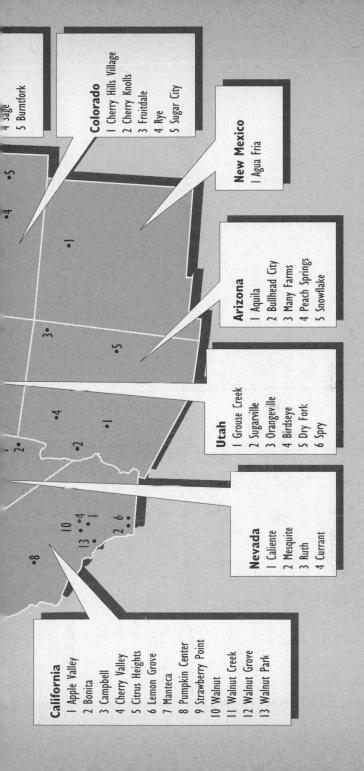

4 Sage
5 Burntfork

Colorado
1 Cherry Hills Village
2 Cherry Knolls
3 Fruitdale
4 Rye
5 Sugar City

New Mexico
1 Agua Fria

Arizona
1 Aquila
2 Bullhead City
3 Many Farms
4 Peach Springs
5 Snowflake

Utah
1 Grouse Creek
2 Sugarville
3 Orangeville
4 Birdseye
5 Dry Fork
6 Spry

Nevada
1 Caliente
2 Mesquite
3 Ruth
4 Currant

California
1 Apple Valley
2 Bonita
3 Campbell
4 Cherry Valley
5 Citrus Heights
6 Lemon Grove
7 Manteca
8 Pumpkin Center
9 Strawberry Point
10 Walnut
11 Walnut Creek
12 Walnut Grove
13 Walnut Park

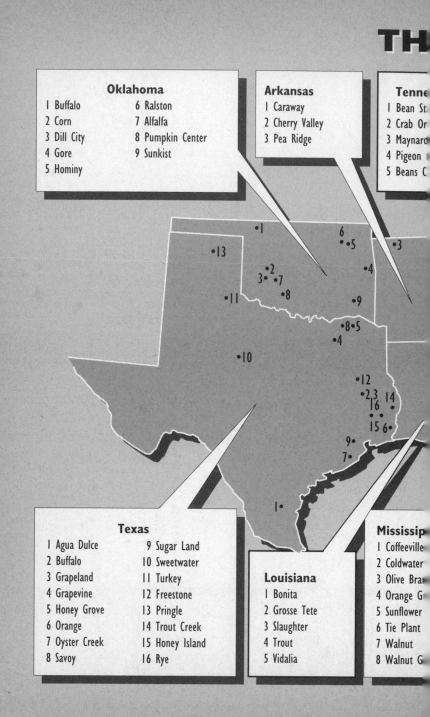

TH

Oklahoma

1 Buffalo	6 Ralston
2 Corn	7 Alfalfa
3 Dill City	8 Pumpkin Center
4 Gore	9 Sunkist
5 Hominy	

Arkansas

1 Caraway
2 Cherry Valley
3 Pea Ridge

Tenne

1 Bean St
2 Crab Or
3 Maynard
4 Pigeon
5 Beans C

Texas

1 Agua Dulce	9 Sugar Land
2 Buffalo	10 Sweetwater
3 Grapeland	11 Turkey
4 Grapevine	12 Freestone
5 Honey Grove	13 Pringle
6 Orange	14 Trout Creek
7 Oyster Creek	15 Honey Island
8 Savoy	16 Rye

Louisiana

1 Bonita
2 Grosse Tete
3 Slaughter
4 Trout
5 Vidalia

Mississip

1 Coffeeville
2 Coldwater
3 Olive Bra
4 Orange G
5 Sunflower
6 Tie Plant
7 Walnut
8 Walnut G

OUTH

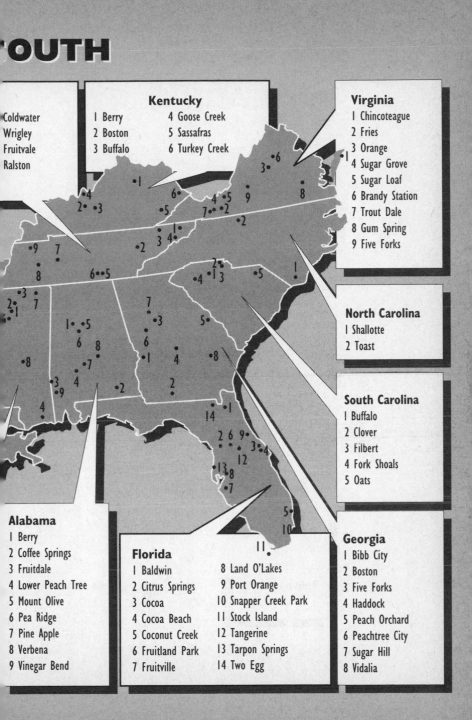

Kentucky

1 Berry 4 Goose Creek
2 Boston 5 Sassafras
3 Buffalo 6 Turkey Creek

Coldwater
Wrigley
Fruitvale
Ralston

Virginia

1 Chincoteague
2 Fries
3 Orange
4 Sugar Grove
5 Sugar Loaf
6 Brandy Station
7 Trout Dale
8 Gum Spring
9 Five Forks

North Carolina

1 Shallotte
2 Toast

South Carolina

1 Buffalo
2 Clover
3 Filbert
4 Fork Shoals
5 Oats

Alabama

1 Berry
2 Coffee Springs
3 Fruitdale
4 Lower Peach Tree
5 Mount Olive
6 Pea Ridge
7 Pine Apple
8 Verbena
9 Vinegar Bend

Florida

1 Baldwin
2 Citrus Springs
3 Cocoa
4 Cocoa Beach
5 Coconut Creek
6 Fruitland Park
7 Fruitville
8 Land O'Lakes
9 Port Orange
10 Snapper Creek Park
11 Stock Island
12 Tangerine
13 Tarpon Springs
14 Two Egg

Georgia

1 Bibb City
2 Boston
3 Five Forks
4 Haddock
5 Peach Orchard
6 Peachtree City
7 Sugar Hill
8 Vidalia

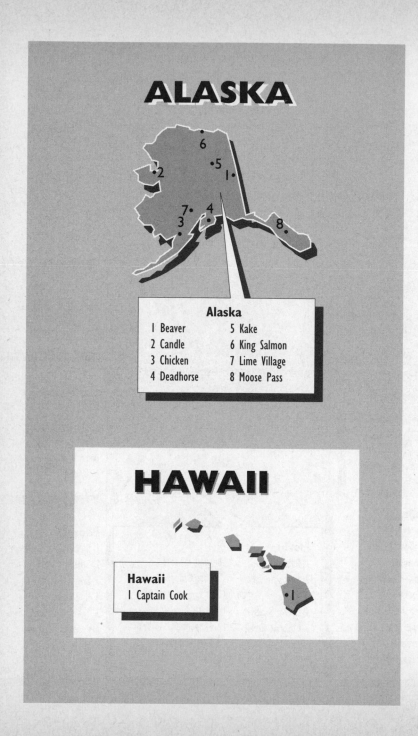

ALASKA

Alaska

1 Beaver	5 Kake
2 Candle	6 King Salmon
3 Chicken	7 Lime Village
4 Deadhorse	8 Moose Pass

HAWAII

Hawaii
1 Captain Cook

ABOUT THE AUTHORS

CHRIS MAYNARD, a corporate and editorial photographer and noted cookbook author, lives in San Francisco with his Airedale puppy, Pluggy. He sincerely hopes that this book will raise his political correctness. If not, he happily accepts the consequences.

He blames nothing on his parents.

BILL SCHELLER is the author of eighteen books and serves as a contributing editor for *National Geographic Traveller*. He lives with his wife and young son in northern Vermont.